DISCOVERING
HOME
—WITH—
Laurie Smith

Meredith® Books
Des Moines, Iowa

DISCOVERING HOME WITH LAURIE SMITH

Editor: Vicki L. Ingham
Assistant Art Director: Erin Burns
Copy Chief: Terri Fredrickson
Publishing Operations Manager: Karen Schirm
Senior Editor, Assets and Information Manager: Phillip Morgan
Edit and Design Production Coordinator: Mary Lee Gavin
Editorial Assistant: Kaye Chabot
Book Production Managers: Pam Kvitne, Marjorie J. Schenkelberg,
    Rick von Holdt, Mark Weaver
Contributing Copy Editors: Kristin Bienert, Jane Woychick
Contributing Proofreaders: Julie Cahalan, Beth Havey, Nancy Ruhling
Principal Photographer: William Stites
Contributing Photographers: Blaine Moats, Laurie Smith
Photostylist: Diane Carroll
Indexer: Sharon Duffy

MEREDITH® BOOKS
Executive Director, Editorial: Gregory H. Kayko
Executive Director, Design: Matt Strelecki
Senior Associate Design Director: Mick Schnepf
Marketing Product Manager: Tyler Woods

Publisher and Editor in Chief: James D. Blume
Editorial Director: Linda Raglan Cunningham
Executive Director, New Business Development: Todd M. Davis
Executive Director, Sales: Ken Zagor
Director, Operations: George A. Susral
Director, Production: Douglas M. Johnston
Director, Marketing: Amy Nichols
Business Director: Jim Leonard

Vice President and General Manager: Douglas J. Guendel

MEREDITH PUBLISHING GROUP
President: Jack Griffin
Executive Vice President: Bob Mate

MEREDITH CORPORATION
Chairman and Chief Executive Officer: William T. Kerr
President and Chief Operating Officer: Stephen M. Lacy

In Memoriam: E.T. Meredith III (1933–2003)

All of us at Meredith® Books are dedicated to providing you with information
and ideas to enhance your home. We welcome your comments and suggestions.
Write to us at: Meredith Books, Home Decorating Editorial Department,
1716 Locust St., Des Moines, IA 50309-3023.

If you would like to purchase any of our home decorating and design,
cooking, crafts, gardening, or home improvement books, check wherever
quality books are sold. Or visit us at: meredithbooks.com.

> **Home is a place where we can be silent and still be heard . . . Where we can ask and find out who we are . . . Where sorrow is divided and joy multiplied . . . Where we share and love and grow.**
>
> – author unknown

THIS BOOK IS DEDICATED TO MY LOVING
HUSBAND, BRAD, AND OUR PRECIOUS SON, GIBSON.

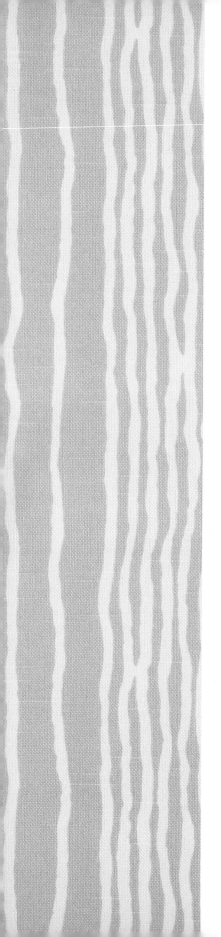

Dear Reader,

Renovation is a discovery process that can bring joyous surprises one day and problematic challenges the next. It's a metaphor for life, I suppose, yet through the challenges we grow, and the happiness that accompanies the finished product usually makes us quickly forget the setbacks.

I know this intimately because last year my husband, Brad, and I renovated a 1950s home in Jackson, Mississippi. Some days we danced with excitement over the possibilities, while other times we were dumbfounded by the problems we uncovered. Regardless, we love our home—so much that we wanted to share it with you.

Please know this book is meant to be a source of encouragement to cheer you on to your own design discoveries. Whether you are building or remodeling a home or simply breathing fresh life into one of your rooms, I hope the chapters excite you for the journey.

If you truly can embrace the notion that an interior is a reflection of the soul, almost immediately there is no room for mistakes or fear. Rooms rooted in inspiration will express their own life and soon nurture you in return.

Certainly a home that brings joy is the ultimate motivation for interior design! My hope is that the journal of my experiences may bring clarity to your path toward *Discovering Home*.

My best,

Laurie Smith

Laurie Smith

Thanks to my family and friends for your steadfast support and continuous prayers. Your encouragement helped me to persevere and see this project through. Thanks to Valerie Summers at William Morris Agency and to Meredith Books, which provided me with the opportunity to write my renovation story. Thanks to Patsy Clairmont, a seasoned writer, who taught me how to begin the book-writing process with a leap of faith. I'm grateful to Bill Stites and Diane Carroll, my photographer and stylist, who viewed things in my home with artists' eyes. Thanks also to Erin Burns, who laid out these pages lovingly, and to Vicki Ingham, who ensured that words and photos worked together; to Bryan Smyda, the talented furniture maker I was blessed to collaborate with—my home is inspiring to me because of his enormous talent; and to Jane Gerber, who transcribed my many scribbles and handwritten notes to create this personal story of *Discovering Home*.

CONTENTS

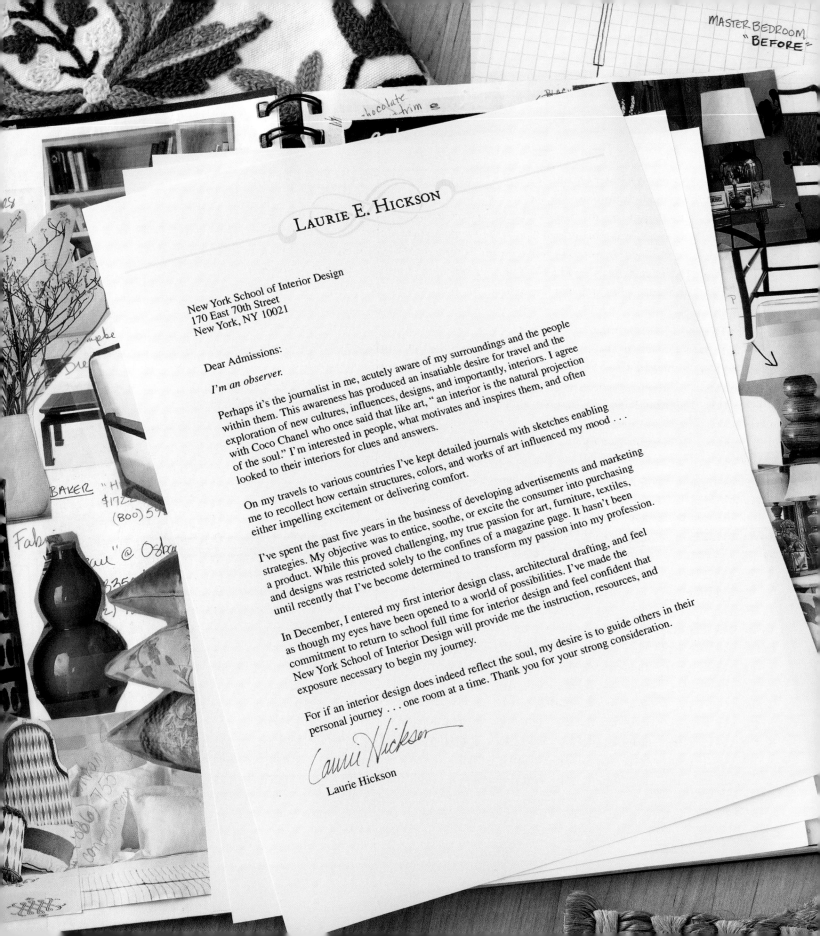

LAURIE E. HICKSON

New York School of Interior Design
170 East 70th Street
New York, NY 10021

Dear Admissions:

I'm an observer.

Perhaps it's the journalist in me, acutely aware of my surroundings and the people within them. This awareness has produced an insatiable desire for travel and the exploration of new cultures, influences, designs, and importantly, interiors. I agree with Coco Chanel who once said that like art, " an interior is the natural projection of the soul." I'm interested in people, what motivates and inspires them, and often looked to their interiors for clues and answers.

On my travels to various countries I've kept detailed journals with sketches enabling me to recollect how certain structures, colors, and works of art influenced my mood . . . either impelling excitement or delivering comfort.

I've spent the past five years in the business of developing advertisements and marketing strategies. My objective was to entice, soothe, or excite the consumer into purchasing a product. While this proved challenging, my true passion for art, furniture, textiles, and designs was restricted solely to the confines of a magazine page. It hasn't been until recently that I've become determined to transform my passion into my profession.

In December, I entered my first interior design class, architectural drafting, and feel as though my eyes have been opened to a world of possibilities. I've made the commitment to return to school full time for interior design and feel confident that New York School of Interior Design will provide me the instruction, resources, and exposure necessary to begin my journey.

For if an interior design does indeed reflect the soul, my desire is to guide others in their personal journey . . . one room at a time. Thank you for your strong consideration.

Laurie Hickson

Laurie Hickson

love reflecting on this letter I wrote to the New York School of Interior Design in 1998 as part of the application process. You see, journalism and marketing had been my prior careers, so it was quite a shift in direction when I made the decision to attend design school. At the time I was working for Turner Network Television in Atlanta while still harboring a childhood dream to perform on the other side of the camera. After shying away from such aspirations, as I had so many times before, I decided it was time to seek a career that would better nourish my creativity.

Good design was something I was blessed to grow up with. My family lived in modest but comfortable homes when I was growing up in Georgia and Texas. My mother made sure each home had distinctive style and flair. While my living environment was important to me, I never had considered design as a career possibility. Then Heather Zarrett-Dewberry, my dear friend and an Atlanta designer, inspired my path. I loved trailing behind her on a Saturday to observe the design process. I had worked closely with creative directors in the marketing world and gained an understanding of color and composition. Coupled with an art history background from Southern Methodist University in Dallas, Texas, and additional studies and travels abroad, this exposure to the design world ignited my passion for color and architecture. With Heather's encouragement, I began taking drafting and space-planning classes at night. To my surprise, I loved sitting for hours at the drafting table and learning to draw three-dimensionally. My world was changed. It was the perfect time to apply to design school, and where better than New York, the heart of American design?

During my time at the New York School of Interior Design, I met my husband, Brad Smith. He was a Mississippi attorney visiting his artist sister, my friend Elizabeth, in the city. Never did I dream that following my husband to Mississippi would afford me the opportunity to audition and appear as one of the original designers on TLC's hit show *Trading Spaces*. Life definitely can take some interesting turns when you decide to follow your heart.

Five seasons into *Trading Spaces*, I continue to be faced with multiple design challenges. Regardless of the obstacles of budget or room size, I've found myself approaching each space with the same design formula. It's a formula that has worked well in my own home, and my hope is that it will translate into success in yours.

one

UNDERSTANDING THE BONES OF YOUR HOME

For the first four years of our marriage, Brad and I lived in a historic neighborhood in Jackson, Mississippi. Built around a small liberal arts college, Belhaven is an area filled with prewar bungalows, many with characteristic Southern style and flair. Generations of artists have found comfort and inspiration in these colorful streets, including the nationally acclaimed author Eudora Welty, who lived in her Belhaven home until her death. I loved our little house, even with its constant maintenance. The beauty of an older home is that the projects you can't afford to tackle that year can be chalked up to charm and character. Our bungalow had all the qualities I loved: hardwood floors, large windows and landscaped views, crown molding, and ornamental mantels. It was Southern and it felt good. When we took our precious baby boy, Gibson, home from the hospital, this is where we brought him. Certainly, we have many wonderful memories we cherish in that home.

With the addition to our family, however, came the necessity of additional space. When Brad and I first viewed our current home, it was love at first sight—but the love was for the lot, not for the house. I had always heard "location, location, location," and in this instance there was no denying the appeal of the setting. However, this midcentury split-level home was a far cry from our historic Southern bungalow.

Above left: Laurie, Brad, and Gibson. **Above right:** Before remodeling, tiny ribbon windows tucked up under the eaves let in little light upstairs. Skylights added to the deep porch were an unsuccessful attempt to relieve the darkness of the entry. **Opposite:** After a complete makeover, stucco has replaced the cedar board-and-batten exterior and seamed copper sheathes the redefined roofline.

> " In this house **simplicity** was a necessity. I decided to eliminate moldings in favor of a more modern sensibility. "

This is where understanding the "bones" of your home proves important. By bones I mean the shell: a room's floor, walls, and ceiling. The first thing I felt when I entered this house, aside from disliking its darkness, odd angles, and oppressively low 8-foot ceilings, was that the house couldn't breathe. Previous owners with traditional sensibilities had dressed every space with ornamentation that fought the bones of the house. Where clean lines of drywall had once met the ceiling, there were now mismatched lowered entrances with heavy cased openings. Angles that had once effortlessly converged were suffocating in crown molding. All the things that I loved in the old house seemed wrong in the new one, and I quickly realized this house needed freedom—freedom to be itself!

My basic plan was to restore the original character and introduce charm where it was lacking. One important architectural element I looked to for guidance was the staircase balustrade. I surmised the design was original to this 1950s home; its Chinese Chippendale style was popular in that era. The dramatic geometric pattern also had been placed in side windows flanking the front door. Such deliberate and prominent placement of this motif led me to believe this is what the home yearned to reflect. Hence, the motif became my reference in the renovation process. The style of the balustrade catalyzed the mood for the house, and the white lacquered wood against the dark handrail set a tone for the other rooms to emulate. In this house simplicity was a necessity. I decided to eliminate moldings in favor of a more modern sensibility.

Above: The entry sidelights were opaque, heavily frosted for privacy. We replaced them with clear glass to let more light enter. **Opposite:** The staircase in the entry hall provided the key to our remodeling decisions. The design of the balustrade recalls Chinese Chippendale fretwork popular in the 18th century and revived in the 1950s.

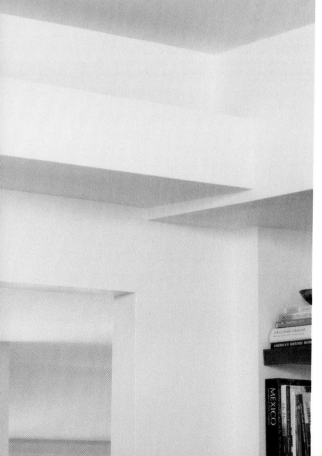

> " The magic of renovation occurs by turning the negative into the positive. "

One must truly study the details of a home to understand its bones. By examining the flow of the rooms and the architectural elements, I began to notice inconsistencies in this house. Mismatched moldings, intruding cabinets, and odd additions appeared as afterthoughts. In some areas rooms seemed to flow into one another, while in others dark hallways interrupted spaces, creating a disjointed effect. I did not have access to the original 1950s owners to ask questions, so I found myself having to work from my gut. I took my cue from original openings, where drywall simply merged with the ceilings—no moldings at all. I began reading about midcentury architecture and learned that the visual axis for residential design was horizontal. Rooms were meant to flow from one to another, creating a feeling of openness. Windows were key elements, and ribbon windows were introduced. (These are horizontal windows that emphasize the sprawling feeling of the 1950s home.) Openness was the goal, and I realized that dark halls did not belong here. I needed to honor the bones of this house and make the space feel as open as I could.

Initially our renovations found us knocking down walls and peeling away layers. At other times we added elements to strengthen the shell. For example, originally the door between the keeping room and the kitchen was off-center, and the wall was disrupted by awkward cabinetry and shelving (see *page 29*). To improve the flow to the kitchen, I centered the opening and had concealed shelving built on each side to create symmetry (see *page 17*).

The opening between the living room and the keeping room also needed attention. When we bought the house, large sliding doors housed on a metal track separated the two spaces. While the doors had quite a bit of character due to their scale and clean ornamentation, the metal track created an unattractive break in the parquet floor, and its division of the spaces made the windows in both rooms seem unbalanced.

Opposite above left: New built-in bookcases replaced the track sliding doors that once separated the living room from the keeping room. We also centered the opening from the keeping room into the kitchen to create an enfilade arrangement (that is, openings between connecting rooms are aligned) to enhance the feeling of openness. Opposite above right: The traditional style of the old mantel suited neither the modern spirit of the house nor the proportions of the room. The new, clean-lined mantel, standing amidst the clutter of construction, seems almost heroic by contrast. Opposite below left: We stripped away accumulated moldings and then raised the doorways to emphasize the clean, geometric planes of intersecting soffits, walls, and ceilings. Opposite below right: Centering the opening from the keeping room into the kitchen required reconfiguring the storage space on each side. The sliding doors were reused here to cover the new shelves.

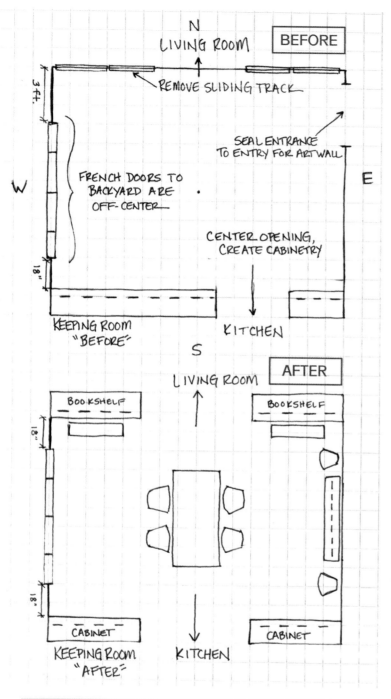

N

LIVING ROOM   **BEFORE**

← REMOVE SLIDING TRACK

3 ft.

SEAL ENTRANCE
TO ENTRY FOR ARTWALL

W   E

FRENCH DOORS TO
BACKYARD ARE
OFF-CENTER

18"

CENTER OPENING,
CREATE CABINETRY

KEEPING ROOM
"BEFORE"

KITCHEN

S

LIVING ROOM   **AFTER**

BOOKSHELF   BOOKSHELF

18"

18"

CABINET   CABINET

KEEPING ROOM
"AFTER"   KITCHEN

Above: Originally the keeping room felt out of balance, with the French doors off-center on one wall and the entry to the kitchen off-center on the adjacent wall. New built-in bookshelves along the living room wall squared up the keeping room so the French doors are now centered on the exterior wall. The wall between the keeping room and kitchen has been reconfigured to center the opening, creating a clean line of sight connecting the three rooms. **Opposite:** The keeping room is a passage connecting the living room and kitchen and a destination, the place where we eat our daily meals.

Opposite: Raising door heights, removing unsuitable crown moldings, and eliminating the track sliding doors restored the open floor plan and sense of flow appropriate to a midcentury house. **Right:** Instead of painting the bookshelves white to match the walls, I chose stained walnut to contrast with the white, taking my cue from the contrast on the balustrade.

In the keeping room, the distance from the left corner of the room to the edge of the window was about 18 inches, whereas the distance from the opposing corner was about 36 inches. This made the keeping-room windows off-center, creating displeasing aesthetic proportions.

To remedy the problem, we removed the sliding track and, with the help of a contractor, constructed a pair of bookcases about 6 inches in from the original position of the track. The 12-inch-deep shelves aided in creating an almost perfectly square floor in the keeping room. Windows and French doors that once appeared off-center are now evenly positioned between the two corners of the room and anchor the space.

My thrifty nature, which has been sharpened by *Trading Spaces*, inspired me to recycle the tall track sliding doors and use them as cabinet fronts in the keeping room and pocket doors into the kitchen. They later served as a template for two additional doors leading from the kitchen to the laundry room and playroom. Using these large-scale doors and raising the door openings created the illusion that the kitchen ceiling is higher than 8 feet.

"

One must truly study the details of a home to understand its bones.

"

The magic in renovation occurs by turning the negative into the positive, or perhaps by reassessing what you view as negative and embracing it as a positive. I do believe a house can acquire good bones if an owner makes smart choices. In our case we reclaimed the bones by paring down moldings and researching midcentury architecture. I encourage you to use books as reference tools when making style choices that pertain to the era or design intent of your home. Hiring an architect also may aid the process. With large renovations, the expertise of an architect or interior designer is a necessity. It is often difficult to detect supporting walls and other essential structural elements. An architect can eliminate much of the guesswork. Trained professionals also can help you make the most efficient use of space.

Above left: The layout of the old kitchen worked well for us, and the cabinets were in good condition. I liked the fact that they continue to the ceiling; the uninterrupted line makes the space feel larger, and there is no space for collectibles or dust to gather. **Above right:** Because vertical elements help make a small space feel larger by drawing the eye upward, we raised the height of the door to the laundry room. **Opposite:** All-white walls, cabinets, and ceiling also enlarge the apparent space in the kitchen, because there are no boundaries to stop the eye. The white setting allows our stainless-steel appliances to stand out.

Our house had another midcentury characteristic we couldn't deny: the parquet floor. Before we fully embraced the bones of our home, Brad and I wanted to replace the parquet with pine planks or cover the floors with wall-to-wall sisal. The wood had been stained so poorly in the past that its species was unrecognizable and, quite frankly, unattractive. It wasn't until we sat down with a decorator friend who knew the history of the house that we learned the floors were teak! What a surprise—what we thought was a lemon was now a jewel. This is a classic example of understanding the bones of your home. Previously we had turned up our noses at the parquet because we were accustomed to more traditional planks of pine; then we decided to embrace and celebrate the original flooring. Instead of covering it up as planned, we stripped and sanded it and applied a protective coat of polyurethane to restore the natural teak hue. The difference is breathtaking. Once again, by accepting the original architecture and celebrating the genre of our home, we were able to uncover a work of art.

Having learned a huge lesson from the floors, we decided to keep embracing elements that were indicative of midcentury architecture, despite the fact that we entered the renovation with more traditional sensibilities. I must admit, having almost made such a grave error, I can understand how natural it is to impose one's personal style on a home, regardless of whether that style coincides with the architecture. It's an innocent mistake that previous owners had made. After I made the decision to embrace midcentury design, I was determined to stay focused. I would no longer consider exchanging modern casement style windows for traditional-style windows with mullions. Eliminating traditional attractive moldings, mantels, and baseboards took discipline because I like them. However, my research proved they did not belong in this house. I would have loved to raise every 8-foot ceiling, but aside from the cost,

I knew the ceiling height in many spaces was deliberately designed with odd angles and pitches. Initially it was not easy to embrace these qualities, but as soon as I did, choices felt more natural. Elements that once appeared unfortunate seemed to shine. Slowly but surely our house was breathing again, resuscitated by the freedom to be itself.

> By accepting the original architecture and celebrating the genre of our home, we were able to uncover a work of art.

Opposite left: At first we did not know what a treasure we had in the parquet floors. They had been poorly stained in the past and through years of wear had become dull and unattractive. Opposite right: When we discovered that they were in fact teak, we had them refinished and restored to their natural hue.

two

EVALUATING YOUR SPACE

The first step in the design process is to evaluate your space. What is the function of the space? Is it a place where many gather to socialize, or is it a personal retreat shared by only a few people at a time? Evaluating the function is crucial to the success of the design. For this step I encourage people to empty their space of all furniture and accessories so they'll have a clear view. It is much easier to envision something new when you are looking at a clean slate. Take detailed measurements of the space, marking the locations of doorways and windows and the length, width, and ceiling height of the room. If there are permanent architectural features such as a fireplace or bookshelves, include them as well. Then begin your evaluation: What do you currently enjoy about this space? When you bought the home, what attracted you to this particular room? Was it the natural light, high ceiling, or wood floors? Or perhaps the space felt cozy, intimate, and comfortable with wall-to-wall carpet. Regardless of your answers, you've completed the first step if you know what you enjoy about the space. Now you can enhance those qualities in the design process.

If positive points didn't occur to you easily, that's fine; it is almost always easier to identify your dislikes. A major part of the process is recognizing what you don't like. This knowledge will help focus your efforts to correct inadequacies in the space. If you have lived in the home awhile, you are one step ahead, because you probably have firm opinions. For instance, if you know that one thing you don't like about your family room is the lack of storage, you can remedy that in the remodeling process. If there is a wall in the living room that is always a challenge to fill or seems cluttered by mismatched shelving units, perhaps you want to consider designing built-in shelving or cabinets—or plan on investing in that armoire you've had your eye on for the last six months.

Do you receive good light in the space? At what time of day is the light strongest? Would you like the windows to drive the design as a focal point for your furniture layout, or would you prefer that they create atmosphere in a more subtle fashion?

continued on page 34

Opposite: Before remodeling, sliding doors on a metal track separated the living room from the keeping room. An off-center doorway and asymmetrically arranged cabinets and shelves filled the wall between the keeping room and the kitchen. Following pages: New built-in bookcases frame the opening between the living room and keeping room, and a new, centered doorway connects the keeping room to the kitchen.

CENTER OPENING

HIDDEN STORAGE

REMOVE SLIDING TRACK

CENTER DOORWAY &
BUILD BOOKSHELVES

DINING ROOM

NEW CHANDELIER

PITCH IN CEILING

SEPARATE SEATING AREA

NEED SCULPTURAL TABLE FOR SQUARE SPACE

In my dining room, the windows, although large, were not a strong architectural feature, because the pitch of the ceiling stunted their proportions. The ceiling started at 8 feet and sloped to about 6 feet above the windows so there was no room to extend the windows upward for a more pleasing look. When I ignored the awkward pitch of the ceiling, however, and measured the walls, they formed an almost perfect square. Square rooms seem to cry out for a round table, and that suited me perfectly—I've always felt that conversation flows more easily at a round table. With no strong architectural features in the space to provide a focal point, a round dining table would become the centerpiece and anchor for the room.

One thing I strongly disliked in the dining room was the north wall, which was adjacent to a dark corridor running from the entry hall to the kitchen. In this wall was a small, awkwardly placed door opening into the hall. By tearing out the wall, we visually extended the dining room and created an open passage to the kitchen. Opening a wall can bring dramatic change to a room. In this case my dining room is now open and bright, and the once-dark corridor has become a cheery passage suitable for artwork.

> " I've always felt conversation flows more easily at a round table. "

Above left: I disliked the way a narrow door connected the dining room to the hallway running from the entry to the kitchen. The corridor felt dark, and access to it from the dining room was constricted. Above right: By removing the wall and opening the dining room to the hallway, we created a dramatically expansive and welcoming new space. Opposite: The hall wall becomes a stunning backdrop for art that can be enjoyed from the dining room. A crystal chandelier replaced the old brass one; it is more in keeping with the light, airy atmosphere of the room.

Opposite: The buffet and chandelier belonged to my grandmother and date to the 1940s. The bistro mirror on the wall above the buffet evokes the same era. Although it's new, it is based on an old design and is made from antique glass. The acrylic lamps are also vintage but look thoroughly contemporary with new white shades. Madagascar wallcovering warms the space with touchable texture. **Above:** The buffet is a 20th-century interpretation of the 18th-century Hepplewhite style. Instead of topping it with traditional porcelain lamps, which would be visually heavy and more formal, I chose clean-lined acrylic ones for their sleek sophistication and transparency. As a result the buffet anchors the wall but doesn't tip the room out of balance.

REMOVE COPPER HOOD

BUILD CABINETS

ADD WINDOWS

BUILD NEW WALL

PLAY AREA
FOR GIBSON

ADD WINDOWS

REMOVE HOOD

INSTALL WALL

SEAL UP CLOSET

GIBSON'S PLAY AREA

When you are considering the natural light in a room, you may realize that the space is simply too dark. This was the case with our casual family room, which we call the playroom. The room had few windows and little light; it was big but had no architectural features or primary focus. In fact, when we bought the house, the space was nothing more than a glorified storage closet. A built-in bar with a copper hood suspended from the ceiling chopped the room into odd spaces. The room lacked a clear layout and seemed ill-suited to accommodate one.

Through the evaluation process I determined that the bar had to go. It was preventing an effective furniture layout, and it had a traditional design that fought the modern lines of the house. Brad and I knew that we wanted this space to feel more intimate, conducive to good conversation or watching a movie. We also wanted it to be a room where Gibson could spread out his toys and play or retreat to his own corner to work at an activity table. Finally, we wanted additional windows and storage.

After playing with the awkward dimensions, I decided to install a wall where the bar had been, creating a storage room. This provided much-needed cabinetry from floor to ceiling and redefined the remaining space to a more manageable scale. To add light, we installed new windows centered in one exterior wall and flanked them with more cabinetry for additional storage. Now toys, games, and a television can be concealed behind doors inspired by a 1940s French standing screen I saw in a magazine.

Above: The playroom was oddly shaped and too big, with too few windows and no architectural focal point. The bar with a copper hood, *center*, took up space and did not match the architecture of the house, so we resolved to tear it out. **Opposite:** New built-in storage and windows transform one end of the room. A chocolate-color wall anchors and warms the room and draws attention to the seating group.

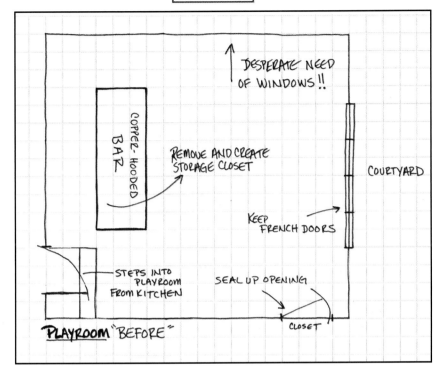

DESPERATE NEED OF WINDOWS !!

COPPER-HOODED BAR

REMOVE AND CREATE STORAGE CLOSET

COURTYARD

KEEP FRENCH DOORS

STEPS INTO PLAYROOM FROM KITCHEN

SEAL UP OPENING

CLOSET

PLAYROOM "BEFORE"

Opposite: The door fronts of the new cupboards were inspired by a French standing screen that I spotted in a magazine. We kept the original tile floor but covered it with a large sea-grass area rug to unify the room and create a cozier feeling. **Left and below:** To remedy the playroom's awkward, ill-proportioned spaces, we enclosed the space once occupied by the bar, pierced an exterior wall with windows, and added a pair of deep, floor-to-ceiling cupboards. **Following pages:** In the master bedroom, French doors in one wall were not enough to keep the room from feeling cavelike. We planned for new windows in the adjacent wall, keeping in mind the placement of our king-size bed on that same wall.

The simple act of adding windows to the playroom transformed a glorified storage closet into a sun-filled, **livable space.**

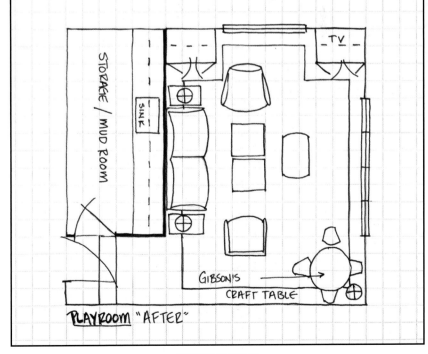

STORAGE / MUD ROOM

SINK

TV

GIBSON'S CRAFT TABLE

PLAYROOM "AFTER"

MASTER BEDROOM

REPLACE FIXTURE

INSTALL WINDOWS

INSTALL WINDOWS

REMOVE CARPET

Our master bedroom was another example of how the evaluation process highlighted the need for windows and light. With little natural light and wall-to-wall carpet, the room originally felt cavelike. We decided to add windows to one wall to increase the light, and we determined their proper placement by taking into account where the king-size bed would be placed on that wall. In choosing the style and size of the new windows, we used the existing French doors as a guide and kept the new windows in proper scale and proportion to them.

We banished the wall-to-wall carpet after we discovered the teak floors in the living areas. Our refinisher, Randy Chapman, seized on the idea of locating a match to the parquet and installing it in the master wing. This would create a seamless transition throughout the first floor. Needless to say, we were thrilled with the result of his pursuit. He was able to locate the match in California and complete our shared vision.

The evaluation process also should take the ceiling into account. Most people prefer higher ceilings because they promote an airy feeling. However, in our midcentury home, many of the ceilings are 8 feet at

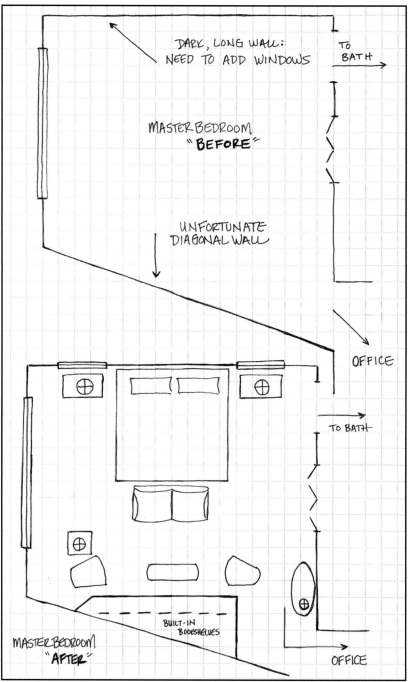

Above left: When we installed new windows, we were careful to keep them in scale with the French doors. These single-pane casement windows suit the midcentury style of the house. **Above:** Placement of the bed guided the positioning of new windows. **Opposite:** Different wood tones can live well together. Here a crewel fabric that contains both dark and honey gold tones brings together the colors of the dark-stained bed and the white oak bedside table (made by Bryan Smyda). The rug also picks up the color of the oak.

their highest point, and the ceiling in our master bedroom is no exception. To address this problem we played with proportion to create the illusion of greater height. For example, by exaggerating vertical elements in the master bedroom, we tricked the eye into perceiving the space as loftier than it really is. Mounting the drapery rod just below the ceiling and allowing draperies to fall in a long column to the floor is one easy way to create the illusion of height. Building floor-to-ceiling bookshelves and adding a chandelier also urge the eye upward, reinforcing the impression of space. A vertical mirror over an oval table and a four-poster bed further enhance the lofty feeling of the room.

Opposite: New built-in glass-front bookcases turn part of the bedroom into an intimate library/sitting area. The vertical emphasis of the doors fools the eye into perceiving the ceiling as loftier than 8 feet. Hanging the draperies just below the crown molding and opting for a bed with tall posts also enhance the illusion of height. **Left:** A tall mirror over an oval table contributes to the feeling of spaciousness by emphasizing the vertical and by bouncing light back into the room. **Following pages:** A new window brought light into the master bath. We salvaged the sinks but built new vanities designed to look like vintage chests of drawers.

MASTER BATHROOM

REMOVE MEDICINE CABINET

INSTALL WINDOWS

INSTALL VINTAGE STYLE VANITIES

Above right: Work in progress: We salvaged the original sinks but had new furniture-style vanities made to flank a new window. **Below right:** Retro faucets evoke a 1950s Atomic Age look. **Far right:** Renovating the bathroom gives you the opportunity to include amenities such as makeup mirrors on adjustable arms.

Simple aesthetic changes also transformed the master bath. A bathroom that was once dark and depressing is now light-filled and spacious-feeling, even though the actual dimensions of the room never changed. We removed the long sink counter and large, horizontal medicine cabinet and replaced them with two separate sink vanities flanking a new vertical window. The window serves a dual purpose, adding natural light and emphasizing the vertical in a primarily horizontal space. The new vanities showcase the original porcelain sinks and hardware that were salvaged in the demolition. Our contractor had the clever idea of building the vanities to mimic 1950s-style chests of drawers. He designed U-shape drawers that fit around the plumbing and provide more convenient and accessible storage space than the usual undersink cabinets.

> " What was once dark and depressing is now **light-filled and spacious-feeling,** even though the actual dimensions never changed. "

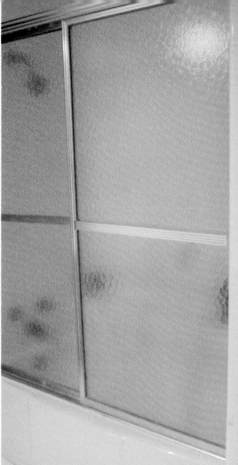

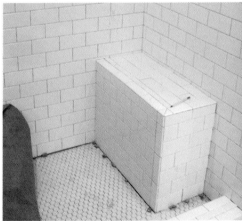

Above top: The old tub and shower with sliding glass doors were thoroughly typical of late-20th-century suburban houses. We decided to opt for 21st-century comfort and replaced the unit with a large shower and seat. **Above bottom:** Work in progress: White bricklike tiles for the walls and seat and white hexagonal tiles for the floor evoke a vintage feeling in the redesigned bath area. **Left:** The new spa-style shower offers a minimalist simplicity that suits our modern aesthetic.

"

Evaluating the function of a space is crucial to the success of the design.

"

HEIGHTEN OPENING

CLOSE OPENING

REMOVE MOLDING

Evaluating the entry hall, we easily identified our goal: to make this space feel as welcoming as possible. Its 8-foot ceiling posed the usual challenge, however. What could we do to draw visitors into the entrance of our home and make them immediately feel inspired? We felt that showcasing artwork in a gallerylike setting was the answer. Quantity of art was not as important as its strategic placement, but the architecture of the space needed to be changed to present the art most effectively. One of the original openings still remained, joining the entry to the dining room. The drywall continued straight up to the ceiling, and this became my template. We changed the narrower opening to the right to reflect the same style and create a monolithic wall between the two openings. It is now the perfect space on which to center a painting. The adjacent wall contained a redundant set of openings into the living room. By sealing one and raising the other, we were able to create yet another important wall to house a large abstract painting full of drama.

Previous pages: We closed the cased opening connecting the entry hall to the keeping room and removed the moldings that framed the opening to the living room. **Above:** Transformation in progress: The original opening joining the entry hall to the dining room continued straight up to the ceiling with no header over the entrance. The shorter, narrower door to the right framed a dark corridor to the kitchen. We raised the height of that opening to match the original one, thereby creating a monolithic wall for featuring art. **Opposite:** The entry now functions as a gallery, showcasing some of our favorite pieces.

66 Showcasing **artwork** in the entry hall draws visitors in and immediately makes them feel inspired. 99

The stairway also helps define the character of the entry. The visual rhythm of the balustrade and the structural regularity of the treads and risers dominate the space, providing the inspiration for the style and mood of the rest of the home. The stair also inspired my choice of a secretary to share the space in the entry hall. The piece emulates the clean lines of the stairway while echoing its light and dark contrasts. It beautifully anchors the corner of the entry.

Evaluating each space in your home helps you decide whether you need dramatic change or a mere face-lift. In our kitchen, for example, there was no need for major structural change.

Above left and right: Previously the entry felt dark and cramped. Now it is a light, bright gallery space showcasing some of our favorite paintings and a sculptural custom bench by Bryan Smyda. **Opposite:** A secretary turns this corner of the entry into a destination in its own right, a sunny spot to make a phone call or take messages. The clean lines of the piece relate to the architecture, while the white finish and black interior repeat the light and dark contrasts of the stairway.

KITCHEN

INSTALL STAINLESS HARDWARE

RAISE DOORWAY

REPLACE SOLID DOORS WITH GLASS PANES

UPDATE APPLIANCES

FRESH COAT OF PAINT

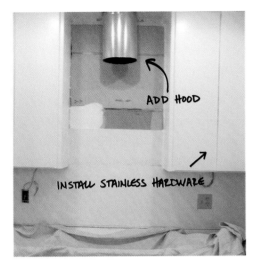

ADD HOOD

INSTALL STAINLESS HARDWARE

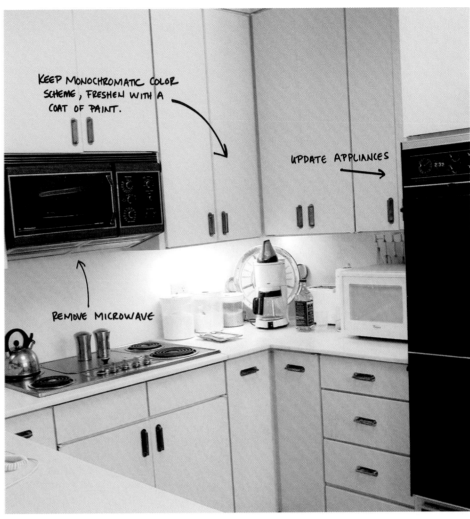

KEEP MONOCHROMATIC COLOR SCHEME, FRESHEN WITH A COAT OF PAINT.

UPDATE APPLIANCES

REMOVE MICROWAVE

Only minor reconstruction was required to widen and heighten two doorways. The existing cabinets were very plain, which suited the space. They were well-constructed and extended to the ceiling, which is an asset in creating the illusion of added height. When cabinets do not go all the way to the ceiling, the space above them breaks the vertical flow—and it becomes a haven for dust and knickknacks. I definitely prefer a clean, seamless look. To refresh the cabinets, we painted them white and replaced the aged-brass pulls with new stainless-steel ones. The hardware harmonizes with the new stainless-steel appliances. To create interest, I also replaced some of the solid cabinet fronts with glass panes. I enjoy collecting fun glassware, and the glass fronts allow me to display my collection while introducing splashes of color in an otherwise white space. I chose single-pane glass to coordinate with the existing casement windows in the kitchen; traditional glass fronts with mullions would not have harmonized with the architectural character of the house.

Above left: Work in progress: We kept the cabinets but removed the wall-mounted microwave and installed a stainless-steel hood and cooktop. Above right: The kitchen as it looked originally. Opposite: Fresh paint and new stainless-steel pulls update the cabinets and harmonize with the new stainless-steel appliances. Previous pages: Cabinets extend to the ceiling, creating a clean, seamless look. We kept the original tile floor, which is durable and easy to clean, but replaced some of the solid-front cabinet doors with glass to enhance the sense of space.

PUT CABINET DOORS HERE

MOVE PHONE JACK INSIDE DESK

CHANGE HARDWARE ON HINGED PULLOUT DESK

FIND TALLER STOOLS

MAKE INTO FILE DRAWERS

This page: The kitchen originally had a shelf unit and drawer beside the counter. For a cleaner appearance, we covered the upper shelves with doors and converted the lower shelves to drawers. Because part of the counter can be seen from the keeping room, I chose substantial, well designed barstools that give the eye a pleasing place to rest.

three

DETERMINING YOUR LAYOUT

eople often ask me what I think is the most important part of the design process. I tell them absolutely, hands down, the furniture layout. The layout is the foundation of the design. If furniture placement and the traffic patterns around it are not correct, the design will not be successful, no matter how beautiful the fabrics and accessories are. It is amazing how merely rotating a chair can make an impact.

MAXIMIZING YOUR SPACE THROUGH LAYOUT

Make your living spaces mirror your lifestyle. Is this the room where your family spends the majority of its time, or is it a room that is frequented only by guests at occasional parties? If it's the latter, I encourage you to consider dual purposes for the room. For instance, to enhance the livability of our dining room, I knew it needed to serve an additional purpose besides eating. The end of the room had a wonderful large window with a great view that was rarely being enjoyed. To remedy this I created a seating arrangement in front of the window, a spot where guests can enjoy an after-dinner drink and where I can sit with a girlfriend and have coffee any afternoon. By placing a furniture grouping in front of the window, we made the dining room a place we could use on a daily basis for reasons other than fine dining.

Opposite: The dining room usually is used at night for special meals, but the garden views deserve notice during the day. To give this room more than one purpose, we furnished the area alongside the windows to serve as a comfortable spot for coffee and conversation. Look for ways to maximize your use of space in any room by carving out areas that can serve multiple functions.

Left: Bergére chairs that stood in the sitting room in our former house were too dainty in scale for the living room of the new house. **Opposite:** In the master bedroom, however, these chairs are perfect for defining a library area in front of new built-in glass-front bookcases. **Below:** The sunburst mirror found a new home over our bed.

Imagine multiple uses for each living space in your home and ultimately you will have rooms that are lived in, not just furniture showrooms that are never used. I provided for multiple uses of space in our master bedroom, my office, the living room, and the entry. My husband is an avid fiction reader and loves to collect books, especially signed first editions. Because our home had limited shelving, I had to be creative in finding a place where Brad could keep his books protected and displayed. Our master bedroom was an awkward, large, dark addition built at a 45-degree angle from the existing home. New windows remedied the natural-light deficit; however, we still were left with an uninviting space lacking intimacy. This is the opposite of how a master bedroom should feel. To create a comfortable bedroom retreat, we needed to maximize the space, devising an intimate floor plan that would encourage multiple uses. Because book collections bring warmth to any room, this was the perfect opportunity to create a place for Brad's library, along with a comfortable place to sit, read, and visit. With the aid of a finish carpenter, we designed and built a glass-front bookcase that simultaneously squares up the room and introduces the intimacy the space had lacked. Now furniture that once resided in the sitting room of our Belhaven bungalow has a new home near the bookcase at the foot of our bed.

> **While I designed my office to accommodate my needs, I also wanted to be sensitive to my husband's occasional use of the space.**

My office is another space that serves a dual purpose. While I designed the room to accommodate my needs, I also wanted to be sensitive to my husband's occasional use of the space. When we purchased the house, he had only a few requests, one being a good working kitchen (he's the chef) and the second being a spot away from the main living spaces where he could place the chair of his choice to read in solitude. Now the question was, which chair and where? The logical place was my office, and because my husband has a great eye, I knew I would like his choice of chair. My office is now a room we both can use comfortably.

Opposite: The placement of a single piece of furniture can define how a room feels. Instead of aligning my desk with the wide wall of my office, I placed it perpendicular to that wall. As a result the room feels pleasantly full and balanced, and I have a nice window view. **Above:** My husband's reading chair and its side table are icons of modernism, as are my desk chairs. The sleek lines and metal surfaces capture the spirit of the house itself. Even the desk accessories maintain the look of simplicity.

" **Furniture layout is the key to a successful design.** "

Other examples of multifunctional spaces are the living room and entry hall. The living room needed to accommodate at least eight people for conversation or watching television. I also wanted a place other than my office where I could sit and write a letter, pay bills, or sketch. Placing a writing desk in one corner of the living room fulfills that need, and the chair provides extra seating for guests when we need it. Now, when I choose to, I can work in the living room instead of being confined to my office or to the kitchen table, which always seemed to be my sole work surface in our previous home. The entry hall also contains a secretary. The piece provides room for display and a quiet place to write a note or talk on a cordless phone, away from the kitchen.

DEFINING TRAFFIC PATTERNS

Taking traffic patterns into account is crucial when you are determining your furniture layout. If one room serves as a passageway to another, you must allow for easy traffic flow as you position furniture to serve the function of the room. This was definitely a challenge in our keeping room, which is really our casual family dining room off the kitchen. Because our kitchen is strictly a working kitchen, we needed a place to sit and eat everyday meals.

An old French farm table stands in the center of the keeping room. This table is special to us because Brad and I found it when we were traveling in Provence, France. It is made from one solid plank of elm and is more than 150 years old. Centering the table allowed enough room on each side to pull out the chairs and provided space for traffic to move through the room. This placement also permits easy access to the French doors, through which Gibson runs in and out to play.

Another area where traffic patterns were vital to the furniture layout was the playroom. This room receives more traffic than any other because we use the French doors daily as we go to and from the garage. The furniture arrangement needed to stay clear of that path while promoting conversation, television watching, and Gibson's freedom to play.

Above: We wanted to showcase this antique farm table because it was one of the treasures we found on a trip through Provence. Opposite: The enfilade arrangement of rooms means that the keeping room doubles as a passage between the kitchen and living room. Centering the table in this room allows plenty of space for chairs to be pulled out and leaves paths for traffic.

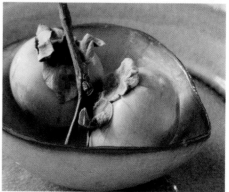

A traffic path should be as wide as a hall—at least 3 feet. To allow enough space, we placed a sofa and two chairs on one side of the room and Gibson's play table in the opposite corner. The table balances the seating group (see *pages 94–95*) and anchors the play area. All goals are met, and plenty of space remains to spread out toys on the floor.

CREATING YOUR FLOOR PLAN

Once you have identified the traffic paths through a room, you are ready to draw up a floor plan. I encourage you to take your time with this step. First, purchase graph paper, a ruler, pencils, and a good eraser—you'll need it, I promise. Next look carefully at the architecture, noting the size, location, and condition of all doors, windows, walls, floors, and ceilings. Is your space symmetrical? If there is a fireplace, is it centered? Are there oddly placed windows or doors? Note these things in

your floor plan because if renovation is not an option, furniture placement can disguise architectural flaws.

Is there an obvious focal point such as a window with a view, bookshelves, or a fireplace? If not, you can create a focal point with furniture. For example, our keeping room had an old farm table and wonderful art, but no true architectural focus. To remedy this, we collaborated with furniture maker Bryan Smyda to design several pieces for the room. One was a walnut glass-front cabinet that stores my porcelain collection and establishes a focal point. Two others, a pair of consoles, flank the doorway to the living room, providing wonderful balance when seen from the kitchen.

Above left and right: A handcrafted glass-front cabinet remedies the lack of an architectural focal point in the keeping room and showcases my porcelain collection. Opposite: Custom-made consoles frame the opening to the living room.

Occasionally I encounter homes where symmetry is lacking. For example, a fireplace may have a window on one side but not on the other. A pair of chairs flanking the fireplace can create symmetry in this situation, as can a mirror or piece of art hung on the blank wall to balance the window.

Always consider the different vantage points in a room and what each visual axis will reveal. It was important to find a focal point for the view into the living room from our kitchen. The blank white wall at the end of that axis needed an attractive anchor, and eventually I placed an armoire there. Looking in the other direction, from our living room into the kitchen, you see the backs of the barstools, so I chose chairs with clean shapes and solid backs to give the eye a place to rest. Walk around your home and notice where your eye lands as you stand in different places. If a hallway abruptly ends with a blank wall, place a console or chair there for visual interest. If you see into a room, place something there to draw the eye. From our entrance hall, for example, one can look through the dining room all the way to the playroom. I placed an attractive table and lamp in the playroom corner to provide a destination for the gaze (see *page 86–87*).

Furniture is the most visible element of any space and is the foundation for the ambience of a room. Use a variety of wood tones, mix traditional and modern furniture styles, and vary heights and shapes to create excitement and interest. Choosing a variety of warm, light, and dark wood tones keeps a room from feeling stagnant. When mixing pieces from different design eras, however, use similar wood tones to make them live together more easily. In my living room a 1940s French end table resides beautifully with a traditional French writing desk in a similar wood tone. Although the pieces differ in

Mixing furniture styles and wood tones creates a layered, collected-over-time look that makes a room visually exciting. An antique armoire anchors one end of the living room, and a traditional French writing desk stands at the other. In between is a mix of modern and traditional pieces that are unified by similar wood tones. Upholstery in closely related colors also helps the various styles live together more easily.

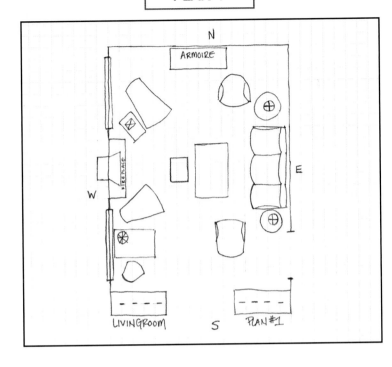

PLAN 1

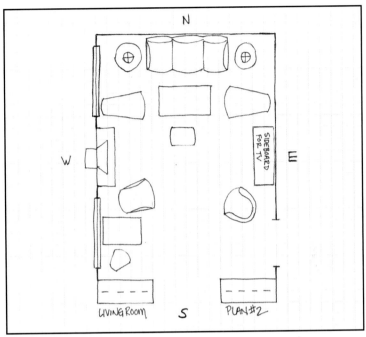

PLAN 2

style, the wood tones unite them. When you become more confident about mixing pieces, wood tone is not as crucial as scale and shape. For example, in my living room, the traditional writing desk relates visually to a blond 1940s end table beside the sofa because both pieces have curvilinear shapes. The curving legs of the end table also are mirrored by the legs of the ottoman and armchair, while the rectangular top of the writing desk is echoed by the rectilinear 1940s side table near the fireplace.

To begin playing with floor plans, measure and record the width, depth, and height of your existing furniture. Are there pieces that can move from one room to another? Draw shapes to scale to represent your furniture, cut them out, and try out different room arrangements on your room sketch. (This is where the graph paper comes in: Let each square equal 1 foot and draw your room dimensions and architectural features to scale.) This process could take hours or days, and that's fine, because a floor plan is the ultimate space-planning tool. Walk away from it and revisit it. If your room is large enough, create more than one seating area. This can be achieved by placing chairs around a sofa in one area and flanking a love seat with two more chairs in another. Or perhaps a pair of chairs can form its own grouping by a fireplace, while a set of chairs congregates around an occasional table off to another side of the room. There were many possibilities for our living room, but I vacillated between only two. I chose Plan 1 in the end, partly because it was my initial solution, and I usually end up going with my gut feeling. Plan 1 also accommodated the large French armoire I had purchased at an auction years ago. Because of the low soffit on the east wall and the fireplace on the west wall, there was no choice but to house the 8-foot-tall armoire on the 9-foot-tall north wall. The height and scale of the armoire add drama and focus, exuding a feeling of grandeur in a not-so-large room. At the same time, the above-the-window drapery installation, a mirror over the mantel, and floor-to-ceiling bookshelves opposite the armoire offer other high points to balance the height of the piece.

Opposite: Similar wood tones connect the 1940s French end table and the traditional, French-inspired chair. Above: To determine the best furniture layout for your room, play with it on paper. At least two different plans could have worked for my living room, but Plan 1 accommodated the armoire, a dramatic focal-point piece I wanted to showcase.

Opposite: Make each vista a beckoning destination. I positioned an interesting floor lamp and Gibson's table and chairs in the playroom at the end of the hall off the entry to anchor that view. **Left:** A blank wall opposite the entry is the ideal spot for a table, a painting, and a pleasing composition of objects.

Challenge yourself to be more of a curator than a decorator when choosing furniture. Instead of buying everything from one or two stores, spend time looking for uncommon objects. Our guest bedroom mixes an antique spindle bed that belonged to my husband's grandfather and new end tables from a furniture store. The clean-lined square tables nicely complement the more ornate bed. I kept the wood tones similar because this is a tight space and the uniformity is less distracting than contrasting wood tones would be. However, I did not want to purchase a console from the same furniture line for fear that the bedroom pieces would begin to look like a suite—ordinary rather than individual. The curator in me looked for other options. I was pleasantly surprised to discover that a console from our old house fit perfectly between the two windows. Its demilune shape was a natural companion for my grandmother's 1950s oval mirror. It took several months to find a slipper chair to suit the space. I found many I liked, but they lacked the back height I needed to balance with the height of the bed. With so much wood in the space, a small marble-top iron table next to the slipper chair provides visual relief with its contrasting texture (see *page 121*). With little extra effort, this guest bedroom feels more curated than decorated. The pieces are of disparate styles, yet there is harmony in their scale.

Opposite: Look for pieces from a variety of sources to create your own confident look. The bed belonged to my husband's grandfather, Gibson, our son's namesake. The mirror belonged to my grandmother. With pieces like these as the foundation, we could add new tables and lamps and repurpose pieces from our old house, such as the console under the oval mirror, to create a room that is comfortable yet rich with character.

> "
> ## Challenge yourself to be more of a curator than a decorator when choosing furniture.
> "

Left: A new bedside table partners well with the antique spindle bed because both have a similar dark finish. The straight lines and simple shape of the table contrast in a pleasing way with the curves of the bed and bedside chair. Note the mixture of prints on the bed. You can successfully mix prints if a common color links the various fabrics.
Opposite: Tulips and a vase in an orangey color add a touch of healthy tension—an element that wakes up a room through unexpected contrast. When colors relate but don't exactly match, the results are livelier, fresher, and more interesting.

Below: Until I can find the perfect chest, this skirted table will serve as an end table for the sofa and chair in my living room. **Right and opposite:** In our old bungalow, the club chair wore a traditional miniprint. Now, dressed in a zebra-print fabric, it brings fresh personality to our current home.

Once you have planned your furniture placement to scale, you've reduced your chances of purchasing mistakes. Shopping with your list of dimensions will make you a more educated consumer, and the search process becomes a treasure hunt. You will no longer purchase furniture in the hope that it will suit your space but rather seek furniture you know will complete the room. In our living room I decided to live temporarily with a skirted table beside my sofa. This is not to say I dislike the skirted table, but I would rather have a beautiful chest of drawers there. The dimensions of the space dictate that the chest be at least 38 inches long. I would rather live with the skirted table than buy a chest of drawers that is not proportionally correct, so I remain on the lookout for the perfect piece. When I find it, the table skirt will be turned into pillows!

In some cases you may already have the perfect piece for a spot, but perhaps it needs a face-lift to fit your new layout. Update old furniture with a fresh coat of paint—white can give a piece a sculptural quality, while high-gloss black brings incomparable drama to a room. Reupholstering is another way to extend and refresh the life of a piece. A large comfortable club chair and ottoman from our old living room were covered in a green leaf pattern; now they wear a fun zebra pattern, taking on a whole new look in our playroom.

that space. If your house contains several fireplaces and you float a sofa in front of each one, your rooms may feel redundant and boring. When making furniture choices, remember that too much matching is a sign of decorating insecurity. Throw in an odd chair or table. Don't be overly concerned with pairing things up. Occasional asymmetry keeps your rooms pleasantly off balance. For example, two different end tables may flank a sofa. If you are moving or remodeling, consider using furniture in a different room than you did before or using it in a totally different context. The living room furniture from our old traditional bungalow makes the perfect seating arrangement in the master bedroom of our new home (see *pages 48–49*). The scale of the pieces is daintier and more in proportion to the 8-foot bedroom ceiling.

If you want to make a large space feel cozier, hang a wide chandelier or boldly shaped light fixture in the middle of the ceiling. If vast rooms are unusually tall, create a horizontal line at eye level with furniture heights and art. If you are struggling to place furniture in a palatial space, several small groupings will create intimacy. Rugs are also a good tool for creating unity in a large space. For example, placing one large sea-grass rug in the playroom drew the space together. It would have made sense to leave Gibson's play area bare in case of spills, but I like the way the rug links that corner to the seating arrangement.

Be deliberate in your furniture placement. Balance upholstered pieces with some that are not upholstered. One of my design school teachers said, "Don't let your rooms become a forest." In other words, beware of too many wooden legs. Soften some of them with skirts. On the flip side, too many skirted pieces can make a room feel heavy. The goal is to strike a nice balance.

Remember, each room is a separate project. Furniture scale and layout that seem appropriate for one space are not always acceptable for another. Take your time and remain aware of how rooms relate to each other. Push yourself to create a different floor plan for each room according to your needs for

Opposite: Using one large sea-grass rug in the playroom unifies the large space and makes it feel more intimate. **Above left:** In Gibson's play area, we applied cork to the entire wall so we could use it as a bulletin board. Then we covered the cork with Madagascar wallcovering for a dressier finished appearance.

LIVING ROOM

LS

AMBER GLASS

CELADON FABRIC
w/ CHOCOLATE
PIPING

ARTISTIC FRAME
"NEPTUNE CHAIR"

STACK
TRAY ON TOP
" SISAL SQUARES"

VLADAMIR VACHIN

THINGS TO DO:

① MEASURE ROOMS TO HAVE BOUND
② REPLACE SHADES ON CRYSTAL L
③ DETERMINE WALL COLOR
   LOOK UP CHOCOLATE BROWN
   ("FRIAR'S ROBE")
④ ORDER G. SMITH SOFA
⑤ ORDER HALL LIGHT FIXT
⑥ ORDER MANTLE MIRRO
⑦ ORDER CFA'S ON
⑧ GET TEAR SHEETS
⑨ INVESTIGATE HINSON
⑩ CA REGARDING C
⑪
⑫

GODARD

GODARD

BRYAN TO BUILD
CONSOLES BASED
ON 1940s
DESIGN

BRYAN TO BUIL
SHELVING UN

KEEPING ROOM

To make a room seem larger, cover the floor with one area rug that leaves a 16- to 18-inch border between its edges and the walls. Because of their transparency, clear acrylic or glass cocktail tables and end tables are an unobtrusive way to make a space feel larger than it really is. Leave about 16 to 18 inches between a sofa and cocktail table to prevent bumps to the shin. Allow about 1 to 2 feet between other pieces of furniture for comfortable passages. In tight spaces, adopt the less-is-more approach and pare down your furniture groupings. Side chairs or ottomans can always be pulled in from other rooms when you need additional seating.

Left: To help you visualize your rooms, use your collage pages, floor plans, and furniture templates to create sketches like these. My sketches help me focus on new pieces I might need to shop for and allow me to check the distribution of shapes and colors around the space.

> FURNISHING YOUR ROOMS <

Don't try to put too much furniture in a room. Without space between pieces, furniture shapes lose importance, and you can't appreciate their silhouettes.

Display antique pieces as if they were sculpture.

Build a room with pieces you love. I would rather have a room that develops slowly over time than one filled with furniture I'll tire of within a couple of years.

Avoid impulse purchases. Remember, faddish fashion passes; good style remains.

The expense of well-crafted furniture is an investment.

Above: Leave enough space around furniture and accessories to create strong silhouettes. In the living room, the smooth, simple lines of this 1940s end table show up well against the white walls. The lamp echoes the table's curves, which repeat in other pieces to set up a visual rhythm around the room.

four

FINDING YOUR INSPIRATION

Determining your layout may be the most critical step in the design process, but finding your inspiration is the most soulful. For centuries artists and other creative types have turned to objects, places, and even experiences to catalyze their creative process. Some artists, like many designers, draw inspiration from others in their field. I once read a quote from a well-known designer who said, "Designers who think they are uniquely original in their construct have no memory." This is so true! As I design pieces of furniture to have custom-built, I am influenced by earlier styles. My furniture maker, Bryan Smyda, is a very talented craftsman who takes inspiration from Sam Maloof, a highly respected contemporary American woodworker.

I deferred to many midcentury designers when looking for ideas for our 1950s home. This is not to say that there is no such thing as an original interpretation; however, even van Gogh's *The Starry Night* was inspired by the night sky in Arles, France, where the artist lived.

Place yourself in the mind-set of an artist, and the design process becomes exciting. When you approach the design of a space by starting with an inspirational piece, this creates a point of reference that you can be passionate about. If you are working with an interior designer, show the designer something you love; this will aid him or her in the preliminary phase of the project. The inspiration piece also can give the designer a reference point to stay in touch with your desires for the space.

Right and opposite: Gibson's bedroom furniture originally belonged to my father when he was a child. Its clean, no-nonsense lines and golden color provided the cue for the custom-built bookcase that furniture maker Bryan Smyda crafted. The piece has a lighthearted look that suits Gibson's room now, but it's also streamlined and modern enough to be appropriate as he grows older.

A good way to start the design process is with an idea file or book. I have both. In design school I began an idea file, a file box divided into subfiles into which I inserted magazine photos ranging from living rooms, bedrooms, and color combinations to specific coffee tables I liked. My file box has nearly 30 categories, which keep me organized; I rarely find myself flipping through stacks of design magazines searching for that "really great lamp." I've dipped into this file countless times for inspiration on *Trading Spaces*.

For my own home, I slowly began to transfer photos that I especially loved into a spiral-bound book. Rooms began to take shape in the pages of my book, and I made sketches as ideas came to mind. This book also traveled everywhere with me as I collected pieces for my home. It held my floor plans, dimensions, and notes to keep me on track as well as contact numbers and websites. I loved watching the pages of my inspiration book fill with layers of photography and color. As I assembled various furniture styles, accessories, and art, color palettes took form, and unexpected schemes began to evolve.

You can learn much about your design style through this technique. You will see themes emerge in the various types of furniture and fabric you are drawn to, and your collage will become as individual as your own handwriting. The scale, the play of positive and negative space on the page, and the simple fact of the way you layer images and ideas can indicate whether you like clean lines or a more organic space. If your collages take on an eclectic nature, that may indicate that you prefer a balance between the two. Your book will help you form a better idea of your own preferences, and it can reveal volumes to a designer if you hire one. If you have not collected files of photography, start now. Look through design magazines, cut out photos that appeal to you, and paste them into your spiral-bound pages. There is no right or wrong way to collage things you like. Just have fun! An idea book is merely a tool for your personal reference.

FINDING SOURCES OF INSPIRATION

Where does one find inspiration for designing a space? You may find it in one of the photos from your collages or in an object, such as an heirloom vase your grandmother gave you as a wedding gift. I recall a *Trading Spaces* episode from our first season when I was asked to describe my inspiration for a color palette I used in a dining room in Philadelphia. This was uniquely memorable for me because it was not an object or a photo that had inspired my palette but rather an image from my memory bank.

On a crisp fall evening at sunset, my husband and I were in a New York cab headed for one of our favorite restaurants in SoHo. The light was so vivid as it reflected off the buildings that for a brief moment I saw a stunning composition of two buildings, one brick red and the other a creamy color with glossy black accents. I turned to my husband and said I had just seen the most regal combination of colors that would make a fantastic dining room! I was responding to a fleeting vision of light and color, but inspiration does not have to be so intangible.

Above: My idea files, filled with magazine photos, are divided into about 30 categories. Opposite: In planning the design for my home, I began to transfer my favorite photos to a spiral-bound notebook. Each page became a collage of colors, patterns, and styles, and unexpected themes emerged.

Parcel

USING THE INSPIRATION PIECE: A CASE STUDY

The more personal your inspiration is, the more meaningful your space will become. When Gibson was about 9 months old, Brad and I took a vacation to the Provence region of France. In addition to a farm table for our keeping room, we found some beautifully carved pears. Each one was hand-turned by a gentleman in the hilltop village of Moustiers. While this particular village is famous for its faience ceramic ware, these extraordinary pears captured our attention. We sifted through baskets of them, picking out our favorite woods, each indigenous to that region of France. My personal favorite was the olive, or *olivier*. The pears are beautiful and unique, and better yet, they have a happy memory attached to them. They became the perfect inspiration for the keeping room, where our family eats daily meals around the farm table.

So now what? How do you build from there? I asked myself why the pears had attracted me. I realized I loved their simplicity and clean lines and was drawn to their vertical form and warm wood tones. The lustrous wood exuded warmth, and the various grains offered distinct contrasts, some quite light with severe dark tones in the stems. These qualities gave me my starting point. Translating them into a plan for the keeping room meant designing a space that would feel streamlined and simple, with a few dramatic furniture pieces that would contrast with each other in tonal value (darkness versus lightness). At the same time, I would need to accentuate the vertical while maintaining a sense of warmth, much like my pears.

The primary furniture piece would be our farm table. I wanted it to be the heart of the room, centered in the space and aligned with the living room and kitchen openings. The only seating would be the chairs drawn up to the table—my floor plan showed that there wouldn't be room for additional seating because I needed at least 3 feet behind each dining

Above: The French farm table, a souvenir from our travels, is the heart of our keeping room. **Opposite:** The hand-carved wood pears were the inspiration piece. Their vertical form, clean lines, and warm wood tones guided my choices of fabrics and furniture for this room. The chairs are also French, with the same honey-gold patina as the table. Upholstering them in a modern print gives them a fresh, contemporary look.

chair for pullout room and heavy pass-through traffic. (The keeping room is the most accessible travel space between the kitchen and living room, and the French doors to the backyard are used on a daily basis.)

I realized that the most logical spots for additional furniture in the room were the two partition walls leading into the living room. Here I could address the need for contrasting tonal values inspired by the pears. Working with furniture maker Bryan Smyda, I designed two consoles to fill these spaces. They are based on a 1940s French piece that I'd seen in a book. The design also mimics the inverted mitered construction of the living room mantel, subtly linking the two spaces. Taking a cue from the dark stem on the pears, I chose wenge, a dark African hardwood, to contrast with the warm tones of elm and walnut in the other furniture pieces.

Along the eastern wall of the keeping room is a soffit that carries necessary ductwork (see *page 80*). The change in ceiling height posed a challenge for furniture placement, so I decided the best solution was to design a glass-front cabinet to fit under the soffit. This would supply the vertical element suggested by the pears and provide needed storage, turning the awkward space into a display niche.

Left: The aged-gold finish on the sconce offers a subtle sheen similar to that of the carved pears. **Far left:** The design of this custom-built console is based on a 1940s French piece. The wood is wenge, a dark African hardwood; its nearly black finish grounds the medium-brown wood tones. **Opposite:** A glass-front cabinet provides storage and a focal point for the room, displaying a collection of porcelain. Its clean lines were inspired by the verticality of the carved pears.

The search for chair fabric was fun, especially when I came across the citrus print. The fruit motif and warm tones resonated with the wood pears, and the hand-blocked fabric possessed the same character of craftsmanship as the carved fruit. With gold and green as dominant colors, the fabric would blend seamlessly with color schemes in adjacent rooms.

The next thing to address was the lighting fixture. I planned to suspend it above the long, narrow farm table, and I wanted to accentuate the rectangular lines of the piece. Looking for the right fixture became the ultimate treasure hunt. Our search ended in New York, where Brad and I found a fixture that was proportionally perfect and suited the space aesthetically. It has an Asian quality that exudes simplicity and its shape mirrors the soffit; the white portion blends with the ceiling and walls while the black base echoes the color of the wenge consoles.

The economical and durable choice for floor covering was sea grass. With a toddler in the house, there will be spills, and this was an easy-to-clean, inexpensive alternative to a woven wool rug. Sea-grass rugs can be custom-sized, and the material is natural and warm, much like my inspiration—the pears. The wall space above the consoles was the perfect home for two pieces of abstract art, both by one of my favorite artists, Gabriel Godard. These images of Provence introduce shocks of color and add a layer of personal meaning to the room as well. Lastly, I chose white for the walls to serve as a blank canvas and nice contrast to the color and warmth. Now I have a room that I love, inspired by a set of objects I cherish.

The most exciting part of decorating in this way—starting with something you love—is that your inspiration piece is unique to you and so your rooms will reflect your personality in an intimate way. On the following pages are more examples of the inspiration pieces that guided the designs for our home.

Opposite: The citrus print was a happy find. It's hand-blocked, and the shapes are slightly irregular, somewhat like the hand-carved pears. **Above left:** The pears vary in tone and grain according to the type of wood used for each one. **Below left:** The perfect light fixture for this room mimics the architectural lines and horizontality of the soffit and repeats the dark notes of the pear stems and console tables.

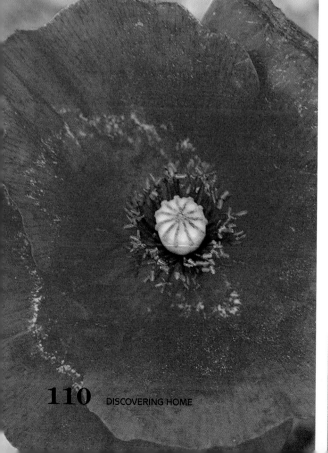

" An inspiration piece creates a point of reference you can be passionate about. "

INSPIRATION PIECE: A MURANO GLASS SEASHELL

In the living room, a Murano glass seashell inspired the mood and amber color scheme. I love the graceful lines of this dish, and its restful quality is reflected in our space. White walls mimic the outer shell, and golden flecks in the glass also appear in the gold color of an accent mirror and drapery rods. Other restful colors were chosen accordingly.

INSPIRATION PIECE: GRANDMOTHER'S CRYSTAL CHANDELIER

In the dining room, my grandmother's crystal chandelier inspired the design. We wanted to pay homage to its 1940s glamour with elegant fabrics, a French bistro-style mirror, and vintage acrylic lamps. Wolf Kahn's *Overall Orange* introduces an unexpected shock of color (see *page 171*).

INSPIRATION PIECE: PATTERNED RUG

This wonderfully patterned rug was an inspiring foundation for the master bedroom. Its expansive dimensions unified the space so pieces from our previous living room did not feel separate from the bed and nightstands. Bronze tones in the rug are highlighted in the beautiful crewel drapery.

INSPIRATION PIECE: CUSTOM DESK

In the office a custom desk drove the design. Inspired by a 1950s Robsjohn-Gibbings original, the desk has an X-shape base and straight lines that set the tone for clean-lined shelves and sculptural furniture. Brown walls are a rich backdrop for the maple-hued piece.

INSPIRATION PIECE: OVAL MIRROR

In the guest bedroom a 1950s oval mirror inspired the design direction. Its gold-leaf frame added a needed sparkle to the bed and draperies. Gold tones are repeated in the fabrics, which guided the choice of warm bronze for the walls. The result is a simple yet elegant room.

INSPIRATION PIECE: GABRIEL GODARD PAINTING

In the playroom a Gabriel Godard painting of fishermen titled *Pêcheurs* provided the starting point. Its playful colors inspired complementary fabrics. Flea market lamps turned into a real treasure with the addition of new drum shades. Comfort and color reign in this space.

INSPIRATION PIECE: CREWEL FABRIC

In Gibson's bedroom Mississippi artist Albert Smathers drew inspiration from this crewel fabric featuring jungle animals. Staying true to their character, he transposed them to Gibson's walls to create a sensational mural. The accent fabrics and designer rug are perfect companions for the furniture, which belonged to my father when he was a child.

five

DISCOVERING COLOR

When I think about color theory classes I had in design school, my most vivid memory is of sitting at my drafting table in my studio apartment mixing various colors of paint. My instructor believed that a designer should have as intimate a relationship with color as an artist does. Therefore, gouaches, which are opaque watercolors, became our medium of choice. They were easy to mix, and we could create brilliant hues with minimal effort. I acquired a true understanding of tonal value through trial and error; although projects could be tedious, they ultimately gave me a skilled eye for colors and how they relate to each other. I began to seek out interesting color palettes in my daily walks around Manhattan. Sometimes my most insightful strolls were through the flower markets; I was acutely sensitive to how nature produced some of the most fabulous color combinations. The view outside my studio window was especially pleasing in the fall as a ginkgo tree turned vibrant yellow against a Prussian blue awning on Third Avenue. Light played an important role in my appreciation of color as well, because the origin of all color viewed in the world is light.

Before designers can communicate color, they must learn a system of color identification. The color wheel, *below*, shows 24 basic colors in their proper relationships. Primary colors—red, yellow, and blue—are the most dominant. Secondaries are the combinations of any two primaries: orange, a combination of red and yellow; green, a combination of yellow and blue; violet, a combination of blue and red. Tertiaries are secondary colors mixed with any additional quantity of one of their constituent primaries. Examples of tertiary colors are plum, a blue violet; mulberry, a red violet; russet, a red orange; flame, a yellow orange; citron, a yellow green; slate, a blue green. Students of color must learn to recognize three qualities in every color sample: hue family, the position on the color wheel; tonal value, degree of lightness and darkness; and chroma, the degree of purity, intensity, or saturation.

Right: The color wheel shows the basic relationships between hues and can help you narrow your choices in creating color schemes for rooms. Successful combinations are based on contrast (hues from opposite sides of the wheel) or coordination (hues that lie next to each other on the wheel). Contrasting, or complementary, colors intensify each other. Coordinating, or analogous, colors harmonize. Opposite: Yellow lemons and shades of yellow and yellow green in the painting are the start of an analogous color scheme.

The color wheel is a starting point for exploration. Color preference is personal, so trust your choices. While your friend may find red exciting and bold, you may find it is unnerving or irritating. Go with your instincts. Only you can decide which colors you are willing to live with in your home.

One way to discover which color combinations you like is to collect paint store color samples and cut them into individual chips. Move the chips around until you find pairs or groups that please you. If you're not sure where to begin, start by combining colors from opposite sides of the color wheel or those adjacent to each other on the wheel.

The color wheel helps you understand frequently used color combinations. To apply the combinations to your rooms, it is helpful to subdivide a room into main areas (floor, walls, and ceiling), secondary areas (large upholstered pieces and window treatments), and minor areas (side chairs, lamps, throw pillows, and other accessories). In a complementary color scheme, two hues from opposite sides of the color wheel are used for the main and secondary areas. These hues generally are repeated in stronger chromas in the accent or minor areas. I've found the use of exact complements (blue and orange, for example) less pleasing than using opposite colors that are slightly tinged with the same underlying hue. For instance, a yellow green harmonizes well with a yellow-tinged red—the yellow is the common denominator between the two complements. In our playroom complementary violets and yellows play well off each other. Accents of citron share the yellow hue and add vitality to the combination.

It is fun to experiment with chromatic distribution in a space. For instance, a more traditional space tends to have mostly neutral values in the dominant areas, while accents take on more chromatic intensity. In more dramatic settings, the most intense values are used on the main areas, while accents become more neutral. There are no exact rules, however. I prefer to experiment both ways. Keep in mind that when two

Opposite: Magenta orchids in a yellow vase exemplify a complementary combination. As the more saturated color, magenta plays up the flowers as a small but powerful accent in the room. **Above:** In the playroom cream and chocolate hues provide a neutral backdrop for a combination of violets and yellows. Small doses of citron, orange, and green in the fabrics share the yellow element and enliven the scheme with warm and cool tones.

> Only you can decide which **colors** you are willing to live with.

Left: Designing my fabric collection for Hancock Fabrics involved visits to the New York offices of manufacturer P/Kaufmann. Opposite: I had fun playing with tertiary color schemes, pulling hues from the entire color wheel into warm and cool palettes. I drew on a repertoire of vintage patterns and played with them, resizing, recoloring, and reinterpreting them for today.

complementary colors, such as blue and orange, are juxtaposed, they will heighten the intensity of each other. Many modern artists deliberately place complements together to take advantage of the increased vibrancy. White, gray, and black need not be counted as extra colors in a basic scheme. Their neutrality lends unity and provides an excellent backdrop for vibrant high-key colors. My color-theory teacher emphasized that every space needs a touch of black for anchoring and contrast. I find chocolate brown to be in the same category, and hence I chose it as a backdrop to make the complementary colors in our playroom sing.

When developing my fabric line for Hancock Fabrics, I produced many patterns that fell into analogous color schemes. These are limited to two or three adjacent hues on the color wheel. A scheme from the warm side of the wheel may include colors ranging from a yellow orange to a coral red. The cool side encompasses green, blue, and intermediate steps between those colors.

A monochromatic scheme is a one-hue plan confined to a single color family. Variety comes from your choices of tonal and chromatic values. A monochromatic scheme works effectively in either a traditional or a contemporary setting. The living room in our previous home was monochromatic in the gold family, varying from light to dark tones. The scheme translated well in the master bedroom with only slight modification: I introduced a small amount of sage with a crewel fabric; because the sage had the same tonal value as the gold, the monochromatic effect was maintained. To preserve a tranquil feeling in the room, I kept the chromatic intensity of the gold somewhat muted. To create a more vibrant space, I would boost the dull gold to a brilliant gold, possibly in accent pillows, for energetic bursts of color.

A monotone space is even more tightly focused than a monochromatic scheme: It is composed of one hue, tone, and chroma throughout. Monotones are usually neutrals, which serve as an unobtrusive background for showcasing other colors and materials. The closest thing to a monotone space in our home is the kitchen. This room is not a large space and has a standard 8-foot ceiling. To give the room a loftier feel, we decided on a one-color scheme with varying shades of white that are similar in tone and chroma. In this setting the eye has no place to rest, so it perceives the space as more open and airy. We raised the doors to the ceiling to add to the illusion of height. White cabinetry and trim seem to fuse into the white

Opposite and above: A monochromatic scheme pulls together a range of light and dark tones from one color family—here, a range of golds, including ocher and brown. The note of sage drawn from the crewel drapery fabric has the same tonal value as the gold, so the room still enjoys the tranquil effect of a subdued monochromatic combination.

> **"Monochromatic schemes work well in either a traditional or a contemporary setting."**

countertops and white walls. Because this is a small working kitchen, we wanted the focus to be on the stainless-steel appliances. Their sleek, modern design takes on an almost sculptural quality in this otherwise simple space.

The study of color is fascinating, and I often have turned to some of my favorite artists for inspiration. Wolf Kahn, one of the most revered artists of the late 20th century, shows no fear when placing bold color fields on his canvases. I admire his freedom and intensity and seek to learn from his example.

Color, in all of its characteristics of hue, tone, and chroma, is a powerful tool in interior design. I once heard an interior designer compare the placement of color to a jazz concert: If separated, the notes seem somewhat off, but together there is harmonic composition. I love this analogy and encourage you to have fun composing your own concert. Whether the end result is warm and inviting, restful and serene, or bold and dramatic is a personal choice, and you control the outcome.

Opposite: I don't believe in matching artwork to the decor of a room, but I do draw color inspiration from some of my favorite artists. Wolf Kahn's subtle layering of yellows, ochers, violet, and pale blue in the landscape painting in our dining room imbues the room with sunny warmth. The yellow notes in the upholstery fabric pay homage to the art without imitating it. **Above:** The fabric combines silvery aqua, yellow, and brown for a fresh interpretation of a timeless color pairing, yellow and blue. Our dinnerware nudges the aqua toward green.

> Color ... is a powerful tool in interior design ... the end result ... is a personal choice, and you control the outcome.

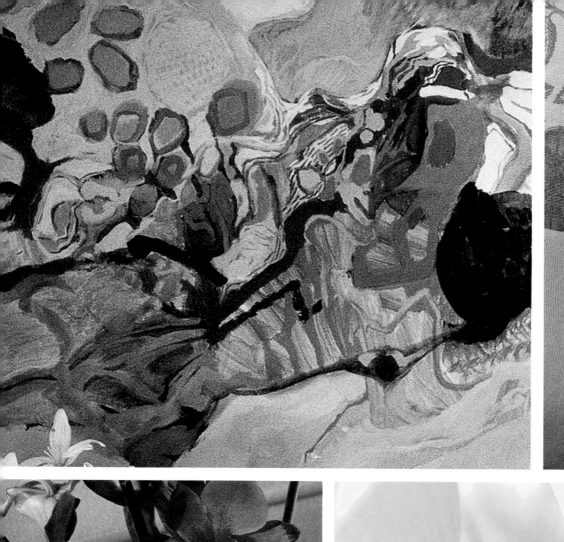

" Have fun composing your own concert of color. "

six

CONSIDERING YOUR FABRICS

After you have determined your layout, found your inspiration, and looked at different ways to use color, it is time to consider your fabrics. If your inspiration piece is driving your color palette, remember to take the item or a photograph of it with you when you shop for fabrics. Of course, a fabric can be the inspiration piece too.

Fabrics are the easiest and most versatile way to introduce color, texture, and pattern to your space. Today's complex market offers every style of textile in a wide price range; whether you favor traditional, transitional, or modern designs, natural or synthetic weaves, you'll find something that suits you. I've worked with fabrics that cost $6 a yard on *Trading Spaces*, and you've all probably seen me splurge with an occasional $75-a-yard fabric for a throw pillow or two. A less expensive fabric is not necessarily less attractive. I've definitely found my share of great looking inexpensive fabrics. However, it is important to evaluate the life span of a fabric. Whether it will be durable and easy to maintain depends on the type of fiber used and the general construction. You may hear people in the industry refer to a fabric as having a good "hand." This means it feels soft, doesn't pill or fuzz, and feels generally stable or durable. Common sense will tell you when a fabric feels flimsy and thin or more weighty and stable. Always handle the fabric you are investing in and ask about its fiber content. One of the most common fibers is cotton. It is truly a staple in the industry. Cotton dyes well, and its durability makes it ideal for both draperies and upholstery. The oldest known textile is linen, made from flax fiber. Linen was used in ancient times—mummies were wrapped in linen cloths. Its hand is crisp, cool, and dimensionally stable, meaning it won't stretch out of shape. It is widely used for table linens, draperies, and even some upholstery. I used a linen-cotton blend on my living room sofa and love the textural look this combination provides. The addition of cotton helps minimize the wrinkling that pure linen tends to show.

Silk is one of the most beautiful fibers available. If you make draperies out of silk, I recommend using lining and interlining, usually a flannel material. While adding lining and interlining means more time and cost for the drapery construction, they are well worth the investment for the preservation of your silk. Without lining and interlining, silk will discolor and ultimately disintegrate from the sunlight. Additionally, the linings add body and weight to the drapery. Heavier flannel interlinings are known as "bump" in the trade.

Opposite: A print in gold ocher hangs at the living room windows, making an organic counterpoint to the geometric prints on the chairs. Simple pinch pleats allow the hand-blocked linen to hang neatly from a custom-made "antiqued" gold rod and rings.

When considering fabrics for upholstery, check the selvage (the tightly woven side edges of the fabric) to see whether the material contains a soil- and stain-repellent finish. (The selvage also often states the manufacturer, fiber content, and colors used, whether a print or woven.) I recently had to have a fabric for my home treated with a soil repellent. It was an inexpensive process and now affords me extra protection against toddler mishaps. Your upholsterer may be able to refer you to someone in your area who does this. Many retail upholstery fabrics have been treated to resist stains.

How do you build fabrics into your design scheme? When selecting decorative textiles, you need to understand the subtle balance between variety and unity, contrast and similarity. Fabric gives you the opportunity to introduce varying textures and patterns, which add personality and flair to your space. Traditionally, fine silks, damasks, and brocades were the fabrics of choice for formal settings. However, combining rough and satin textures makes an effective modern statement. For example, upholstering dining chairs in a natural woven fiber that resembles burlap or raffia and using silk for the draperies creates an extreme contrast that is stylish and edgy. I used a less extreme contrast in our master bedroom, where I combined linen-velvet, silk, and a crewel fabric. While the linen-velvet and silk are a more expected combination, the crewel, which consists of embroidered wool yarns on cotton, could be considered more casual. The addition of a cotton piqué on the bed adds to the contrast in textures; however, because the piqué has a slightly more sophisticated weave, it resides well next to a pair of silk chairs. The combination of textures keeps our bedroom from feeling as formal or traditional as it would with all silks and linens. The space embraces traditional style with a modern sensibility (see *pages 45–49* for additional views).

Opposite and above: Fabrics for the master bedroom include linen-velvet, silk, crewel, and cotton piqué. The rug contributes to the palette of textures too.

Our texture choices in the dining room remain more traditional, with heavy brocadelike cotton complemented by velvet and silk. I found the floral brocade pattern first and I must admit it was love at first sight! The design motif and scale were perfect for my chairs; the colors were appealing and offered a foundation on which to build a scheme. For the two large chairs and ottoman near the windows, however, I decided to use an overall miniprint pattern that would read almost as a solid and not compete with the pattern on the dining chairs. After much deliberation, I decided not to go with gold or green on the window chairs, although either color would have lived well with the floral fabric. Instead, I chose a silvery taupe cut-velvet applied to blue sateen, which tied in with the blue in the background of the floral brocade and highlighted its silver touches. Now with a floral and a miniprint, the space needed some geometrics.

In design school I learned to combine varying patterns to create interest. Often the placement of a curve will enhance a straight line and vice versa. The ultimate goal for mixing organic and geometric patterns is balance. I find it boring to enter a room that has only geometric patterns or only florals. It is much more visually exciting to walk into a room full of floral patterns anchored by striped accents. That is why I chose a silk stripe to make beautiful pillows for the window chairs in our dining room. The stripe has an anchoring effect for the curvaceous floral. Restricting the fabrics to a monochromatic palette allowed me to splash color on the floor with a golden strié wool rug and on the wall with a boldly colored Wolf Kahn painting (see *pages 33 and 35*).

Right: Silvery taupe cut-velvet on a pale blue base reads almost as a solid but has the inviting component of touchable texture. Accessories bring out the silver and blue elements. Opposite: The fabric palette for the dining room plays curvy florals and a textural miniprint against clean stripes and a woven strié. The straight lines anchor the curvy ones. Even the colors and textures of the woods in the room contribute to the overall feeling. Golden hues from the teak floor influenced the choice of a golden strié rug; dark walnut in the nearby entry hall bench links visually to the dark stems in the floral fabric.

" **The ultimate goal for mixing organic and geometric patterns is balance.** "

The playroom fabrics were built around a stripe that was chosen to complement the inspiration piece in that room, the Godard painting. The stripe, which appears on throw pillows, has accents of deep purple, green, and orange. The golden fabric on the sofa has an orange thread woven into the overall pattern, which runs, unusually, on the bias. An animal print covers the club chair and ottoman, adding a bit of fun. The chocolate brown in this hand-painted print later influenced my choice of wall color, as well as a smaller-scale diamond print on the sofa throw pillows. I chose a solid-green cotton twill for a side chair to play up the green stripe on the other throw pillows. This room exemplifies a good balance of pattern and scale and plays on complementary color schemes (see *page 41*).

Above: The key fabric in building a scheme may not be the most prominent in the room. The striped fabric in this accent pillow guided my choice of fabric for the sofa (gold with a thread of orange), solid green for a side chair and pillow, and chocolate brown for accent pillows and wall color. **Opposite:** Brown and cream geometrics and a hand-painted animal print lighten the mood with unexpected pattern.

Another room that achieves a balance among patterns of varying scales is the living room. The first fabric I chose in this space was for the sofa. It's an unpatterned linen-cotton blend—a good neutral to build on. (A benefit of having a neutral sofa is that you can easily alter the look by changing the throw pillows.) Next I selected the drapery fabric, a hand-blocked linen with a medium-scale organic pattern in gold; this same fabric appears on a table skirt to link the drapery to the rest of the space. I chose a larger-scale geometric gridlike print to upholster the two French side chairs. I love this fabric and thought it was a nice balance of color for the draperies. Citron green on a side chair adds punch to the golden hues, and chocolate brown stripes appear on the sofa pillows for contrast. Warm butterscotch leather adds another layer of texture on a side chair and ottoman. Because I love to combine organic and geometric patterns, I felt a floral pattern with coral accents would be an interesting choice for throw pillows on the grid-patterned chairs. While there are many solids, patterns, and textures in this scheme, their similar tonal values work in conjunction with each other. For example, the yellow-green combination of citron, which appears in a pillow, chair, and lamp, is a companion for other golden-yellow fabrics in the space. By combining colors with similar tonal values, I achieve a more restful atmosphere. However, this warm palette still allows the option to add more vibrantly colored accessories if I want a change.

Above left: A solid citron-color side chair adds punch to the golden hues in the living room. Using the drapery fabric to cover a table brings the organic print into the room; the repetition helps unify the space. **Above right:** Golden tones in the fabric repeat in the mirror frame above the mantel. Pillows introduce a coral note that accents the citron and a lively floral design that contrasts pleasingly with the gridlike pattern on the chairs. **Opposite:** The palette of textures for a room includes decorative accessories as well as fabrics and floor covering. See *page 83* for another view of the pattern mix at work in this room.

Another room rich in fabrics is the guest bedroom. We had decided to recycle the draperies from our former living room and use them in this room, so they provided our starting point. The draperies are a warm tone-on-tone stripe silk. With a stripe at the windows and the straight lines of the bed and end tables, the room needed some curves for contrast. I found two versions of an organic pattern that is similar in scale to the stripe and used one for the bed skirt and the other to cover the chair and comforter. Pillows in a stylized floral accent the allover design. In fact, against the small-scale patterns, the flowers appear almost architectural. All the patterns are fairly close in scale and also harmonize with the small scale of the room. While the flowers in the accent pillows are primarily a deep pink, they have a slight gradation of orange in the petals. Orange and pink are analogous on the color wheel and harmonize well, but orange adds a punch of modern color to an otherwise traditional space. One bright orange bolster creates healthy tension in the scheme. "Healthy tension" is a term used by a design school professor who was opposed to monotonous interiors. Placing a bold or odd color in a fabric scheme can sometimes achieve the edge that distinguishes modern spaces (see also *page 88*).

Left: Most of the fabric patterns in the guest bedroom are similar in scale, which allows the floral accent pillows to stand out like an exclamation point. The solid-orange bolster adds an exciting pop of modern color in an otherwise traditional room. **Opposite:** An overall harmony of tone unites a variety of patterns and textures. Using a selection of large, medium, and small patterns in a room is a common approach. However, you really only need a single large-scale and a single medium-scale print for emphasis against a background of smaller prints.

" Placing a bold or odd color in a fabric scheme creates the healthy tension that makes a room sing."

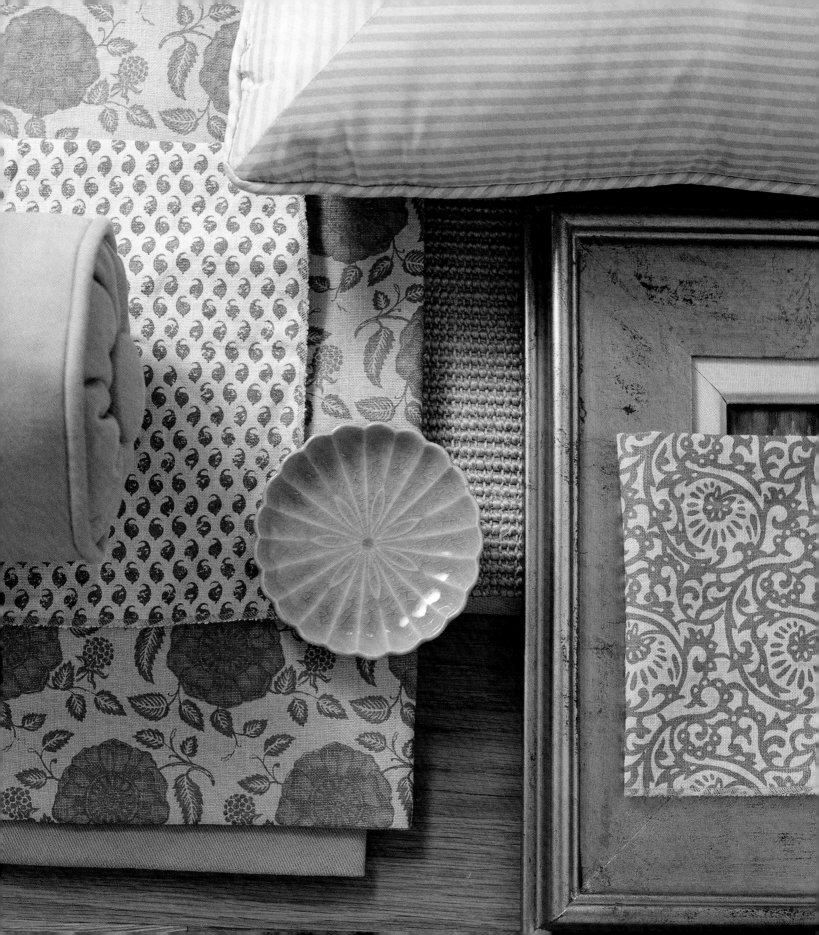

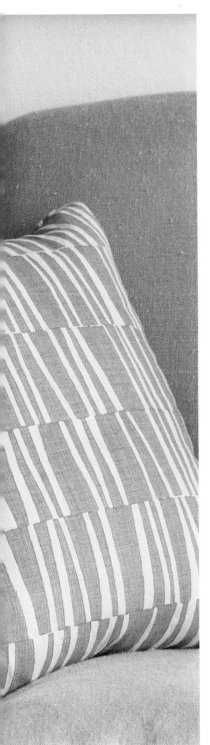

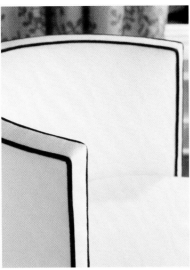

The beauty and color in a patterned fabric can be accentuated by contrasting the pattern with plain fields of color or with neutrals. A single-color fabric makes a backdrop for bold pattern to perform its magic. Solid fabrics also can work magic on their own when enhanced with a contrasting welt cord. Just as placing different colored solids together can be fun, so can placing different scales of pattern together. While patterns of the same scale almost cancel each other out, the contrast of varying scaled patterns can be interesting. That is why I like combining large-, medium-, and small-scale prints when possible. The crucial factor is balance. When mixing smaller- and larger-scale patterns, check the overall look to be certain that none of them dominates. Sometimes a small pattern in a bold color can feel weightier and therefore live comfortably next to a larger pattern. A fabulous pattern can become a focal point for your space. If you fall in love with a pattern that is too expensive for draperies or upholstery, consider buying just enough for making pillows. A dramatic throw pillow can wake up an otherwise drab scheme.

Opposite: Medium-scale prints make cheerful pillows in the living room. The floral offers an organic counterpoint to the geometric patterns. **Above:** Solid welting that contrasts with solid upholstery emphasizes the clean lines and sculptural quality of a tub chair.

> LAURIE'S FABRIC TIPS <

Let fabric inspire you and become the basic foundation for your room design.

Add interest to your space by combining different textures and patterns. Be adventurous with color.

Coordinate colors in your space instead of matching them. Introduce an unexpected hue to create a bit of healthy tension.

Allow geometrics and florals to reside together. Let small- and large-scale patterns play off each other to create personality.

Give your furniture a face-lift with new upholstery or slipcovers. Rotating colorful and patterned pillows creates instant drama. Use down pillow forms for the best shape and comfort.

seven

ACCESSORIZING YOUR ROOMS

Accessories reinforce the overall feeling of your space. The luxury of accessorizing is that it can happen over the course of your life. Accessories may rotate seasonally for a fresh look or remain intact for years. My advice for accessorizing is to seek each object with the same discrimination you used in choosing your furniture. Select pieces that have personal meaning for you or objects that have captured your heart. The details of a room are important; they ought to reflect the soul of the person who lives in the space. Whether it is a lamp or a vase of flowers, each accessory should be placed deliberately. This is especially important with lighting.

LIGHTING

Lighting is possibly the most powerful tool in design. What is the point of investing in furniture, fabrics, accessories, and artwork if you are living in the dark? In design school we learned to view lighting as the most exciting and mysterious medium of design. Lighting transforms the objects it falls on, yet it maintains a mystery, staying invisible until it reflects off a surface. Designers learn how to manipulate light to create desired effects in a space. While there are entire courses dedicated to this one subject, I hope to enlighten you on the basics—no pun intended!

Three general light sources are available in design. The first is natural daylight. Daylight changes throughout the day in intensity and position. Colors throughout an interior are affected by natural daylight; this explains why the same interior can appear dramatically different at night. When you evaluate your space, pay attention to window placement and daylight intensity. These factors will affect how you dress the window and how you position furniture. If natural daylight is lacking, you may need to add a window. In our upstairs landing, enlarging an existing window eliminated further need for recessed lighting at the top of the stairs.

Opposite: The mantel offers an ideal spot for showcasing objects that are beautiful and meaningful. The turquoise vase was a wedding gift to one of my grandmothers almost 75 years ago. The Murano glass pears were part of my other grandmother's collection. A new ocher-color glass vase contributes height to the grouping and helps lead the eye from the outside edge of the mantel down to the pears.

Left: A cube-shape iron lantern with blown-glass panes is a modern classic. **Top:** Lined with chrome trim, the 4-inch recessed can is a modern accent in the kitchen. **Above:** The flame-shape low-watt bulbs are a typical choice for sconces and decorative candle lamps as well as chandeliers. I recommend putting in dimmer switches to control the light level and create an inviting mood. **Opposite:** Table lamps with incandescent bulbs provide both task and ambient lighting.

The second basic light source is incandescent or artificial lamplight—what we generally mean when we refer to a lightbulb. Hundreds of incandescent lamp types are available. Some are general service—the standard pear-shape bulb. Also available are tungsten-halogen bulbs, small in size but powerful, with comparatively long life spans. Decorative bulbs are usually tubular or flamelike in shape and are frequently used in chandeliers. When installing bulbs, use only the wattage recommended for the lamp: A bulb with higher wattage can burst. Unfortunately I have firsthand experience!

The third basic light source is electric discharge lighting, or fluorescent lights. These are low-intensity discharge lamps and commonly are used in offices. In my opinion this light source is not suited for residential interiors. While fluorescent lights do have a longer life expectancy than most incandescent bulbs and use less energy, their color-producing qualities are poor. Warm light cannot be achieved, and as a result the room looks flat with a greenish tinge.

If you are adding installed lighting to your home, consider recessed or pendent lighting. Installing too many recessed lights can turn your ceiling into Swiss cheese, but thoughtfully placed fixtures can have dramatic results. Our art collection guided most of the placement of recessed lights in our home. In the entry hall iris lights mounted flush with the ceiling spotlight art. Their beams are adjustable and wash the paintings in light. For the hallways, we chose recessed 4-inch trim cans, placing them about 2 feet apart. This spacing ensures that they illuminate the passages evenly while casting nice light for future artwork or photography on the walls. The chrome trim on the recessed lights in the kitchen emphasizes a sleek, modern look and coordinates with our stainless-steel appliances and new cabinet hardware.

While recessed lighting is a practical tool for setting a mood in your home, a fabulous light fixture can make a strong design

statement as well as provide illumination. Sometimes the most wonderful thing about lighting is the decorative influence of a single lamp. There are so many shapes, colors, and styles available that choosing can be difficult. To narrow your choices, consider shape and color. Do you want the shape to contrast with your overall room style or coordinate with it? Placing a traditional shape in a modern space adds interest through contrast, while a sleek modern fixture in a traditional space injects a fresh, sophisticated accent. Next, do you want the color to reinforce the palette or recede into the background? A lamp that matches its surroundings will tend to disappear, while a base in a contrasting color can accent the room's color scheme.

Changing a shade can completely transform the look of a lamp. Take the lamp with you when shopping for a new shade and test a variety of styles. Sometimes an unexpected proportion or color produces exciting results. For instance, on my hallway console stands a turquoise lamp I've loved for years; different shades quickly alter the personality and mood of this lamp, *right* and *opposite*.

To determine whether a shade is proportionally correct for a lamp, check that the bottom of the shade covers the socket but does not conceal the top or neck of the lamp. You can lower or raise the shade in relation to the body of the lamp by choosing a different harp size. A shade on a table lamp is best placed no higher than seated eye level, which averages 38 to 42 inches above the floor. Shades on standing or floor lamps are generally above seated eye level; place floor lamps at the rear corner of the chair or sofa they are intended to illuminate.

To allow for flexibility in lighting, equip each room with an adequate number of electrical outlets. If you are remodeling or building, determining your furniture layout early is beneficial,

because the layout may demonstrate the need for outlets in unusual places. For example, if you plan to float a sofa and sofa table in front of a fireplace, an outlet in the floor allows the table to hold a lamp. Similarly, a freestanding chair may need a standing lamp beside it, and a floor outlet will eliminate the safety hazard of a cord stretched across the floor. It's ideal if the outlets can be controlled by wall switches, and if possible, include dimmers. Dimmers instantly can change the mood of a room. Brad and I opted for dimmers, which are quite inexpensive, and the results are transforming.

Above and opposite: I've had this turquoise lamp for years and love the fact that simply changing the shade changes the personality of the piece. The shade, *opposite*, stretches out horizontally for a modern feeling but is still in proportion to the lamp because the seams define the same edge or stopping point as the sides of the round shade, *above*. Thus, although the width is perhaps greater than normal, the seams and angled ends create a visual break so the shade doesn't overpower the lamp.

FLOOR COVERINGS

Floor coverings offer an excellent way to add pattern or color to your space. An area rug can become the focal point or merely serve as a backdrop for upholstery and wall color. In either case, the floor covering has as much impact on the room as the walls do.

The strategic use of an area rug can define a space. Light-color area rugs can make a small space feel larger. On the flip side, a darker rug in a large space can create intimacy and set specific borders for furniture arrangements. Whether furniture stands on or off the rug is up to you; however, if you are trying to make a furniture grouping seem more cohesive, I encourage you to place furniture on the rug. Even if only two legs of a chair rest on the rug, that is enough contact to bring the chair into the defined area. In dining rooms let the chairs rest comfortably on the rug, edging off it only when diners pull them out or push back from the table.

In our dining room, the area rug establishes the boundaries for two seating groups. The upholstered chairs and ottoman stand on the wood floor, while the dining table and chairs are on the rug. I knew the upholstered chairs rarely would move, so there was no danger of damaging the exposed floor; more importantly, I wanted the seating in front of the window to be considered separate from the dining arrangement.

When deciding which size area rug to use, designers often choose one that extends to within 12 to 18 inches of the wall or baseboard. However, this is a matter of personal preference. I allowed 17 inches in most of my living spaces because I love my teak floors and wanted them to remain visible. It is advisable to lay your rugs over a layer of felt or some sort of manufactured pad to add softness and durability. This also helps maintain and protect your floor surface.

If you so choose, your area rug can be the dominant source of color and pattern in your space. In our master bedroom the area rug captures attention with a dramatic pattern, while in other rooms the rugs merely add an accent. Fabric initiated the design in Gibson's room, but the area rug was a key decorative element in completing the design scheme (see *page 178*).

While I do love wall-to-wall carpet in a bedroom, I prefer area rugs in living spaces, simply because it is easier to clean spills and daily traffic stains from wood and tile than from carpet. Sisals and sea grass are my favorites. Easy to customize and less expensive than wool, rugs made of these natural fibers provide a great aesthetic quality while maintaining durability. That is why I chose them for our keeping room, living room, and playroom. Different weaves of these materials provide varying patterns as well.

The floor covering has as much **impact** on the room as the walls do.

Opposite, clockwise from top left: Woven natural fiber contrasts pleasingly with the warm patina of my French writing desk. The woven chenille carpet in the bedroom is luxuriously soft underfoot. A sea-grass rug with bound edges covers the floor in my office. For Gibson's room we chose a handtufted custom carpet of New Zealand wool.

ARTWORK

Artwork is the most exciting part of the accessorizing process. Perhaps it is the influence of my art history background, but to me, art is the means by which drama and personality enter the space. The beauty of art is how personal it is to the owner. Nearly every painting in our home reminds my husband and me of a particular vacation or moment when we stood side by side gazing at a piece. I recall our first art purchase as a married couple in New York. *Yemaya's Bounty* by Tremain Smith (no relation) was hanging at the Phoenix Gallery in SoHo. Brad and I were so moved when we first saw it that we sat on the floor in front of the painting to discuss it. Ironically, our interpretations of the painting were different, but our passion was the same. Now this piece is showcased in our entry on its own wall, *opposite*. If a piece speaks to you initially, you can be certain it always will do so.

The most important advice I can give about buying artwork is never to let your room decor dictate the color palette of your art. If your art matches your room, the result is always stagnant. Art is as individualistic as you are and deserves to be independent of its surroundings. Make sure that the scale of a piece is in proportion to the wall. For example, our living room sofa sits on a long expanse of wall that demands a large-scale piece like the Gabriel Godard, *above*, painted in 1970.

Above: Gabriel Godard's *Neige* hangs above the living room sofa. This energetic painting was based on the artist's dream of an olive orchard struggling to break through a heavy snow. Opposite: *Yemaya's Bounty* by Tremain Smith was our first art purchase as a married couple.

This page: Another Gabriel Godard, this 1969 painting is part of a powerful series portraying the Stations of the Cross. This panel depicts the fifth station, where Simon of Cyrene steps in to help the exhausted Christ carry the cross.
Opposite: This Wolf Kahn landscape, *Overall Orange*, exists independently of the room's color scheme, as artwork should. I hung it on this wall because the scale of the space suits the scale of the painting.

This page: While I never advocate matching art to your decor, the wall color does have an impact on the way you perceive the colors in the art. In our old home *Still Life with Lemons* by Elizabeth Chapin hung against an orange wall, which brought out the blue shades. Here, against a white wall, the yellows dominate.
Opposite: One print would be too small, but a pair of framed Bucci prints centered over the guest bed fills the space and has the impact of a single large piece.

My fascination with the French abstract colorist Godard began when I was in design school in New York. I recall walking past the David Findlay Galleries and feeling my heart literally skip a beat the first time I saw his dreamlike images in the window. I feel blessed to own several of his pieces and believe if you have the opportunity to collect a particular artist, you should.

Wolf Kahn is another master of color whose work never ceases to amaze me. I once heard someone say that Kahn often arrives at an ambiguity in which the figurative and the abstract are virtually indistinguishable from one another. This is exemplified in his work *Overall Orange* in our dining room (see *page 171*) and in *Barn Above a Yellow Field* at the end of our hallway (see *pages 164–165*). Note that the bold color of *Overall Orange* was not placed to match our dining room chairs but rather to exist independently on its own terms. The scale of the painting, however, was perfect for this wall.

Whether you are drawn to traditional landscapes or modern still lifes, let your collection of art develop over time. Become familiar with artists in your city or region. Young talents have to begin somewhere, and often affordable work can be found during an artist's first several shows. You also may be fortunate to have an artist in your family, as we do. Elizabeth Chapin, Brad's sister, was an artist in New York, where she painted our wedding gift, *Still Life with Lemons* (see *page 172*). Now she lives in Austin, Texas, where she has matured into an extraordinary portraitist.

Opposite: A George Nelson clock made for Herman Miller hangs above a small painting of garlic that we bought in Crillon le Brave from a British painter. **Above:** *Payage a Deux Nuage*, painted by Gabriel Godard in 1968, brings bold color to the living room bookshelf. **Right:** Gibson's artwork is thumbtacked to a corkboard wall in our playroom. I covered the corkboard with Madagascar, a popular midcentury wallcovering, and framed it with wood trim to create a wall that is both utilitarian and attractive.

>LAURIE'S TIPS FOR ART<

Always hang art at eye level. In rooms where people are seated, place art at their eye level or lower for surprise.

Allow about 3 inches between frames when grouping your artwork.

Remember, art need not match your decor!

Art is in the eye of the beholder—sometimes a simple hand-painted note card, matted and framed, is a nice touch.

A child's art is always a special adornment.

If displaying photography, find coordinating frames. A group has more impact if the individual pieces have similar mats and frames.

If a piece is too small for a space, group it with one or more pieces to create a composition appropriate in scale.

" Art is as individualistic as you are and deserves to be independent of its surroundings.

"

Canvas is only one medium for art. Consider displaying sculpture or pottery as well. Some furniture easily can be appreciated as sculpture. I consider the pieces made for me by Bryan Smyda to be works of art, as are some of the icons of midcentury modernism that inspired me as I worked with Bryan. The sculptural quality of the chair, *above*, inspired by a Vladimir Kagan design, is a feast for the eyes. The consoles in the keeping room and the bench in the entry have unique designs and are crafted from beautiful woods, wenge and ziracote. The grain of ziracote, a South American wood, is wild, with no regular pattern. Talk about nature as art! You also may choose to treat a mirror as art, as we did over our living room mantel and dining buffet.

Whether hand-crafted or mass-produced, furniture can be so well-designed that it becomes sculptural, an art form you can actually use. **Above left and right:** Bryan Smyda crafted this chair and a matching ottoman from walnut. The design was inspired by the sleek, organic modern furniture of Vladimir Kagan, a key figure in 20th-century furniture design. **Opposite above left:** I took my cue for the design of my desk from midcentury designer Robsjohn-Gibbings. Bryan Smyda built it of maple. **Opposite above right:** This Bryan Smyda bench is a practical place to drop my purse and keys, but its Asian-inspired lines and the dark color of the wood give it the beauty of art. **Opposite below left:** The console, crafted from an African hardwood called wenge, was inspired by a 1940s French piece. The inverted miter design repeats the design of the living room mantel. **Opposite below right:** Butterscotch leather blends with the warm walnut tones of the finished wood.

WALL COLOR

I realize it might seem backward to place wall color in the final chapter of the design process. However, this is precisely where it belongs. I cannot count how many times I have traveled to various locations for *Trading Spaces* episodes and have been faced with the same dilemma: The homeowner says, "I wanted a red dining room, so I painted it red and now I'm stuck!" My reply is always, "You are in this dilemma because you began with the final step!" Always consider wall color to be the ultimate accessory. Only after the furniture, fabric, flooring, and lighting have been determined is it time to consider wall color, trim, and ceiling color. Reversing this sequence forces you to search for floor coverings and fabrics that will coordinate with the established wall color. You can always have a paint custom-mixed to match a color in a fabric, but you can rarely have a fabric custom-printed.

Here is how the process works: You have found the perfect patterned fabric for your living room. You've decided to build your overall scheme on the multiple colors in the pattern. You've found a coordinating stripe and miniprint as well as a few solids. A neutral floor covering has been purchased, and you've found porcelain lamps that echo a color in a painting above your sofa. Now—and only now—can the finishing touch of wall color be determined. Evaluate your art and the fabrics. Is there an obvious color that repeats itself such as blue or green? If so, you may want to place that color on the walls. Or perhaps that is too bold for your taste and you would rather go with a more muted version. As another option, you may consider going with the complementary companion to that color for a dramatic contrast. I love it when the most subtle vein of color in a fabric, such as a cool celadon, coordinates well with the other colors and patterns in a space. In this situation you can pull out that subtle, unexpected color and transpose it to the walls as a backdrop upon which all the colors and patterns in the space can dance!

Above and opposite: A wonderful whimsical crewel fabric inspired the wall murals in Gibson's room. Painted by Mississippi artist Albert Smathers, they prove that color doesn't have to be solid to have impact: These vibrant figures define the personality of the room and introduce color against a background of creamy white.

Always consider wall color to be the ultimate accessory.

For example, in our guest bedroom a gold vein in one of my dominant fabrics inspired the choice of a warm bronze tone for the walls. In my office I chose chocolate brown for the walls because it would be a nice backdrop for the warm maple hue of my writing desk. Chocolate brown contrasts handsomely with my accessories and artwork and also establishes a sense of intimacy in the small space. Dark walls in small spaces bring personality and drama to the room if you have contrasting lighter trim.

White is more than a default choice for wall color. I chose it for several reasons throughout our home. I wanted the drywall angles to appear almost sculptural, and white is the best way to achieve this effect, because it allows no resting point for the eye. We have 8-foot ceilings in many of our living spaces, and white gives our home a more open and airy look. Juxtaposed against rich wood floors, the white walls suggest an art gallery, showcasing the colors of the fabrics, floor coverings, accessories, and paintings. There are numerous shades of white just as there are of any color.

Before choosing a wall color, invest in quart samples of paint and test the colors on poster board—always apply two coats, as you would on your walls—so you can see how each color works with your fabrics and how changing daylight affects the colors. I suggest poster board because painting a new color directly on top of an existing color will alter the appearance of the new color.

Opposite: I chose chocolate brown for the walls of my office to set off the beauty of the maple desk. This is a small room, but the white ceiling, bookcase, and trim ensure that the chocolate color for the walls is dramatic rather than overbearing. **Above left:** The bronze color for the walls in the guest bedroom was drawn from a golden note in the fabrics. **Above right:** For most of the house, I opted for white walls to emphasize the sculptural quality of the architecture and to create a gallerylike background for art.

Sampling color initially will save you the heartache of painting an entire room in a color you don't like. No one can judge a color accurately from a mere paint chip.

Proper wall preparation is imperative for good results. Many walls in our home had cracks and waves that needed skim coating (a layer of drywall joint compound troweled on and then sanded). Also fill nail holes with spackling compound and sand the filled area so the surface is smooth and even. Prime the walls to make a good foundation for the paint and to help it adhere. (Using a tinted primer when painting a deep wall color also may reduce the number of coats needed.) Most interior walls call for latex paint, which demands a latex primer; enamel paint requires an oil-base primer. I'll never forget an early *Trading Spaces* episode when we assumed an existing coat of paint was latex. It was actually an oil-base paint, so although the paint adhered initially, it began to peel as it dried.

Many latex paints can look like and wear like enamel, due to advancements in paint technology. Latex paints with a high-gloss finish are the best choice for woodwork because the gloss finish is durable and easy to clean. A flat finish has the lowest sheen. While this is best for hiding drywall or plaster wall imperfections, it has a chalklike quality that does not hold up well under scrubbing. A flat finish is ideal for ceilings, but for walls I prefer an eggshell finish, which has a slight sheen that allows you to wipe the surfaces clean.

Wallcoverings are another way to bring color to your rooms. On several walls I used Madagascar, a type of grass cloth. This material was used by many midcentury designers so I felt it was appropriate for my 1950s home. Patterned wallpaper can be expensive, but when limited to a small space such as a powder room, it is more affordable and has great impact. The bamboo-pattern wallpaper in our powder room adds sophistication to the blue fixtures, which we saved during renovation. Seaming intricate wallpaper patterns can be a challenge, so you might consider hiring a professional.

Opposite: In the entry hall, I covered the wall with Madagascar, a type of grass cloth that was popular in the 1950s. **Above:** In the powder room, a bamboo-pattern wallpaper has a 1950s feeling that works with the blue fixtures, which we salvaged during renovation.

LAYERING

The layering of decorative objects is another dimension of accessorizing that adds character to a space. In many ways, this is as personal as artwork on the walls. If objects are selected with purpose and love, they always will enrich your home. The beauty of the layering process is that you can pare down groupings or add to them over the years. Be disciplined, however. There is one word I hear often in my field: edit. Taking away an object rather than adding one often will perfect your display. I had a design instructor who suggested this approach: Accessorize your space as your heart pleases; then remove 10 percent. There is much merit to this statement. However, layering is an ongoing process, so it's best to let your displays evolve naturally, without restrictive rules.

When grouping objects on a tabletop, follow the general design rule of working with odd numbers, often just three. This makes it easy to create balance with one object centered and two others as anchors. Experiment with color and scale, but avoid having one object overpower the others. For example, my hall console has two separate groupings with the lamp living independently between the two. To keep the lamp from overwhelming the display, I added a vase similar in scale to the lamp and a stack of books to provide another level of height (see *page 165*).

Above left and opposite: Rely on groupings of three for fail-safe displays. If you have two matching objects, such as the Murano glass pears, introduce variety with a like object of a different size. Shape and color link the antique porcelains, *opposite*, while varying heights create a path for the eye to follow. **Above right:** Layering brings beauty to temporary assemblages too. This is my favorite china, and I love combining it with crystal and silver against the walnut wood of the dining table.

Right: I choose to keep my crystal behind closed doors and bring it out for entertaining. **Below:** In my office fabric samples and reference books are stored on open shelves; the colors stimulate my thinking. **Opposite:** Bookshelves offer the perfect opportunity to practice layering. To emphasize the shelves as an architectural feature, arrange books, objects, and art so that they guide your eye across each shelf as well as up and down the shelves.

Collections are especially wonderful and personal. I happen to love antique and modern porcelain vases. Some are out on display, while others reside in a glass cabinet. At times, some vases may be placed in storage behind solid cabinet doors and then removed for parties or various arrangements. You may choose not to display your collection except seasonally or when entertaining. I encourage this because it adds variety to your space and enables you to appreciate your collection with a fresh perspective. I love to display china and crystal on my tabletop when entertaining, only to pack it away safely in a cabinet afterward. You may prefer to display your china permanently in a breakfront cabinet.

Decorative frames always group nicely in sets of three. One on its own seems lost, but the addition of two others with a similar finish creates a dialogue among them. I've often heard fellow designers refer to the rule of triangulation, the repetition of a color or form three times in a space. In my living room the citron green accent color appears in a sofa throw pillow, on a side chair, and again in a lamp.

Bookshelves offer the perfect opportunity to layer. I love to approach my bookshelves from an architectural standpoint, positioning books and objects in stylized vertical and horizontal stacks. Other times, bookshelves merely may serve their purpose as a library, with books aligned side by side. I love books! They always add warmth and personality to a space. In our previous family room, we chose to encase the sofa in shelves as an architectural statement (see *page 92*). Many of the books and decorative objects we displayed there have found a home on our new shelves in our current living room and in my office. My office was particularly fun to accessorize with storage containers, books, and objects; the shelves achieved an architectural feel with a specific place for everything. Pairs of objects help you achieve symmetry and balance in arrangements on shelves, tabletops, or a mantel. That is why, whether sifting through a flea market or a decorative accessories store, I always look for pairs.

Flowers have special impact as an accessory, bringing a beautiful finishing touch to the layering process. Fresh-cut flowers introduce instant vitality to any space. Wiry ranunculus and twisting French tulips add color and drama, while maple branches cut after the leaves have turned bring the beauty of autumn indoors. Instead of overloading your home with blooms, select flowers carefully and place them strategically to enliven other accessories and to add a jolt of color to a scheme. Potted plants are also a welcome addition and, depending on the plant, can live comfortably in most settings. Keep the arrangement or plant in proportion to its container; logically, taller vases better suit taller arrangements or plants, and shorter stems call for low containers. Use a single flower as a gentle accent and note its quiet impact. The simple task of cutting daylilies and arranging them in a vase can lift your spirits and bring that extra dash of excitement to your space. And remember that the incredible colors in an orchid may inspire an entire room's palette.

Opposite, clockwise from top left: Yellow orchids in a purple vase express the power of complementary colors. Lying opposite each other on the color wheel, each makes the other more vivid. Orange flowers in a pale blue vase also exemplify a complementary pairing, but here the intensities are unequal, emphasizing the flowers. Orange tulips in an orange vase make a monochromatic statement. Succulents bring long-lasting green color to tabletop displays. **Above left:** White hydrangeas practically arrange themselves in a white Italian basket-weave vase. **Above right:** A single flower can have great decorative impact. This orchid in a vintage Haeger pottery vase has the quality of sculpture.

resources/index

Fabrics, Wallcoverings & Floor Coverings

A.M. Collections, Ltd.
979 3rd Avenue, Suite 1700
New York, NY 10022
212-207-8746

Castel
East 57th Street #11a
New York, NY 10022
212-758-9900
www.castelmaison.com

Clarence House (decorative textiles)
www.clarencehousefabrics.com

Edelman Leather Innovations, Inc.
351 Peachtree Hills Ave.
Atlanta, GA 30305
800-367-0481

Peter Fasano
Handcrafted Textiles
964 South Main Street
Great Barrington, MA 01230
413-528-6872

Galbraith & Paul
Handcrafted Textiles
116 Shurs Lane
Philadelphia, PA 19127
215-508-0800

GCO Carpet Outlet
4950-D I-55 North
Jackson, MS 39211
601-982-5423

Hancock Fabrics
Laurie Smith Collection
www.hancockfabrics.com

Hinson & Company Wallpaper & Fabric
718-482-1100

Christopher Hyland, Inc.
979 Third Avenue, Suite 1710
New York, NY 10022
212-688-6121
www.christopherhyland.net

Old World Weavers/Stark Carpet
979 Third Avenue
New York, NY 10022
212-355-7186
www.starkcarpet.com

Patterson Flynn & Martin
979 Third Avenue
New York, NY 10022
212-688-7700

John Rosselli & Associates
979 Third Avenue
New York, NY 10022
212-593-2060

Seabrook (Benjamin Moore Paints)
3019 North State Street
Jackson, MS 39216
601-366-6429

Textiles
584 Broadway
New York, NY 10012
212-625-2616

Travis & Company
351 Peachtree Hills Avenue, NE
Suite 128
Atlanta, GA 30305
1-800-258-2214
www.travisandcompany.com

Watkins & Fonthill
979 Third Avenue
New York, NY 10022
212-755-6700
www.watkins-fonthill.com

Terry Wetzel
(custom rug design, binding, cleaning)
601-291-9164
twetzel@jamrr.com

Accessories

Article
3017 North State Street
Jackson, MS 39216
601-321-1958

Batte Furniture
E. Northside Drive at I-55 North
Jackson, MS 39206
800-366-0338
information@battefurniture.com

Bergdorf Goodman
754 Fifth Avenue
New York, NY 10019
212-872-8719

Crown Hardware (drapery hardware)
133 Wiggins Street
Jackson, MS
601-922-7056

High Street Antique Collection
806 Larson Street
Jackson, MS 39216
601-981-6020

JF Chen Antiques
8414 Melrose Avenue
Los Angeles, CA 90069
323-655-6310
Jchen72105@aol.com

Lisa Palmer Interiors
601-366-2801

Nancy Price Interiors
3110 Old Canton Road
Jackson, MS 39216
601-366-2801

Annelle Primos & Associates
Antiques
Highland Village
Jackson, MS 39211
601-321-1958

United Wholesale Florists
2107 Wightman Street
Jackson, MS 39202
601-353-2731

Vaughan
979 Third Avenue
New York, NY 10022
212-319-7070
www.vaughandesigns.com

Viking Range Corporation
111 Front Street
Greenwood, MS 38930
662-451-4133

Williams-Sonoma Home
www.williams-sonoma.com

Ye Olde Lamp Shoppe
I-55 North
Jackson, MS 39206
601-362-9311

Furniture & Antiques

Artistic Frame
985 Third Avenue
New York, NY 10022
212-289-2100
www.artisticframe.com

Daily-Gromme Antiques
208 King Street
Charleston, SC 29401
843-853-2299

Peter Dunham Interiors
909 N. Orlando Ave.
Los Angeles, CA 90069

Holly Hunt New York
979 Third Avenue
Suite 605
New York, NY 10022
212-755-6555

Lane Home Furnishings
P.O. Box 1627
Tupelo, MS 38802
www.lanefurniture.com

Mayo Furniture, Inc.
1275 Ellsworth Industrial Blvd.
Atlanta, GA 30318
800-241-1648

George Smith
Handmade Furniture and Fabrics
142 N. Robertson Blvd.
Los Angeles, CA 90048
310-360-0880
www.georgesmith.com

Smyda Woodworking
Custom Handcrafted Furniture
Bryan Smyda
P. O. Box 216
Puckett, MS 39151
601-591-0247
www.smydawoodworking.com

Elizabeth Stuart Design, LLC
314 King Street
Charleston, SC 29401
843-577-6272
www.esdcharleston.com

Artists & Galleries
Ameringer & Yohe Fine Art
20 West 57th Street
New York, NY 10019
212-445-0051

Brown's Fine Art and Framing
630 Fondren Place
Jackson, MS 39216
601-982-4844

Elizabeth Chapin, Artist
309 Park Lane
Austin, TX 78704
512-912-8142

David Findlay Galleries, Inc.
984 Madison Avenue at 77th
New York, NY 10021
212-249-2909

Limn Gallery
292 Townsend Street
San Francisco, CA 94107
415-977-1300
gallery@limn.com

Jerald Melberg Gallery
625 South Sharon Amity Road
Charlotte, NC 28211
704-365-3000
www.jeraldmelberg.com
gallery@jeraldmelberg.com

Albert Smathers, Artist/Muralist
2425 Parsons Road
Raymond, MS 39154
601-857-2704; 601-925-32

Tremain Smith, Artist
4520 Locust Street
Philadelphia, PA 19139
215-387-1869
www.tremainsmith.com

Upholstery & Sewing
Classic Upholstery
5310 Old Byram Road
Byram, MS 39272
601-372-9286

Goforth Family Workroom
601-932-3922

Contractor
HomeWorks of Jackson
An affiliate of Kenneth L. Simmons &
Associates
3002 N. Mill Street
Jackson, MS 39216
800-874-2167

Home Construction & Movers
Anthemion
4438 East Ridge Drive
Jackson, MS 39211

Gary Atchley Wallcovering
601-953-8916

Randy Chapman Hardwood Floors
Residential and Commercial
601-847-0992

Comfortech Heating & Air
P.O. Box 12350
Jackson, MS 39236
601-956-3368

Exell Water Treatment Specialists
P.O. Box 5393
Jackson, MS 39296
877-672-8426
www.exellcompanies.com

Garry Graves' Landscapes
2580 Lakeland Drive
Jackson, MS 39232
601-939-5442

Independent Roofing Systems Inc.
601-922-4301
www.roofing.ms

J&J Movers Inc.
420 Meadowbrook Road
Jackson, MS 39206
601-366-9441

Langham's Copper Creations
601-573-1798

Terry Liles, Stucco Specialist Inc.
601-854-6336

Perry Paints
106 Traceridge
Clinton, MS 39056
601-720-1000

Ridgeland Specialty Hardware
320 N.E. Madison Drive
Ridgeland, MS 39157
601-853-3294

index

index (continued)